Mr. Brick & the Boys

a contemporary Western novel

Paul Hunter

Publisher: Davila Art & Books LLC.
PO Box 1627 Sisters, Oregon 97759
541-549-2064

ISBN 1-885210-35-3

Also by Paul Hunter

Sit a Tall Horse (2020)

Clownery (2017)

Stubble Field (2012)

One Seed to Another (2010)

Come the Harvest (2008)

Ripening (2007)

Breaking Ground (2004)

Clown Car (2000)

Lay of the Land (1997)

Mockingbird (1981)

Pullman (1976)

Your House is on Fire and
Your Children Are Gone (1970)

for my brother Jerry

pardners for the long ride

"Grown men may learn from very little children, for the hearts of little children are pure, and therefore the Great Spirit may show to them many things which older people miss."
–Black Elk

"A man that don't love a horse, there is something the matter with him. If he has no sympathy for the man that does love horses, then there is something worse the matter with him."
--Will Rogers

"Depression can't keep up with a man on a good, fast horse."
--Theodore Roosevelt to Seth Bullock

Contents

Getting a Start   7

Fixin' to Settle Down   13

Goodbye to Haze   19

Mud Puppies   23

What Little There is in the Ground   31

Pure Hopeless   39

Whole Lotta Learnin' Goin' On   57

The So-Called Facts of Life   65

Horse-Breaking Rivers   73

Why Don't Horses Laugh   85

The Roundup You Don't Forget   91

Taken for a Spin   97

A Horse of a Different Color   105

Prairie Dog Heaven   125

Flop-Eared Fly-Chaser   137

Boys' Night Out   143

A Likely Spot From Here On Out   157

Hat Christmas   165

No Use Ridin' in the Rain   173

Getting a Start

The spring I got home from Vietnam and mustered out, I moved on. Didn't much like how my dad and granddad were running the old Moon-Dog Ranch as a business. The home place didn't feel enough like the real deal any more, ever since they'd signed up with a big oil company that surveyed the ranch, laid out a grid, and over time methodically drilled and drained what was under all 218,000 acres. Then the two of them mostly spent the money playing cowboys, turned it all into a dude ranch that advertised fun in the saddle, in big cities back east and up and down the west coast. But after a while it seemed like nobody much felt like playing cowboys with all that going on underground. You couldn't see a pump jack from the big house or the fancy new cabins all in a row, but what did that matter? We mighta still had good breeding stock, but even decent horses and cattle could get a little ornery and distracted. The reason wasn't far to seek. You could ride twenty minutes in any direction and catch a strong whiff of the devil.

Grandad and Dad both knew how I felt, but I had saved most of my pay from the Army, and got a job driving schoolbus for the local district from September through June, then helped out the family with the dude ranch over summers for wages. And started scouting land for myself, but it took a while to find any worth a second look. I drove into the city to talk to the VA, then my local bank, and thought I could swing it with a healthy down-payment. The cheapest places were all played out and over-grazed, gully-washed, full of jimson, cactus and tumbleweed. With the realtors it got so every place they showed me had a well full of mud, and a barn roof shot full of holes. Got so they teased me for tasting the water of every well that wasn't bone-dry.

But then I found a lead on my own, in the barber shop of all places. Bernie the barber was completely bald, over sixty and had had a triple bypass, all of which I knew. What I didn't know was that he was looking to cash in and move back to Missouri, which he still called Missoura. While getting my usual haircut at his little place that used to be a two-car garage, I happened to ask him what I asked everyone those days, if he knew of any land for sale. His scissors and comb quit their little clicking dance a minute, and in the mirror I caught his eyes rise up and stare at the ceiling of his little shop, like he'd just heard crickets overhead in the rafters, eatin' a satchel of money. He was thinking of something, but had been cutting my hair a few years, what we'd called loosening my hat since before I went in the Army, so I just waited him out. Eventually Bernie lowered his gaze, studied me in the mirror, and said:

What kinda land would we be lookin' at?

I want to do a little ranching and farming, raise some hay, oats, corn and the like to feed cattle and horses. Need some range land for grazing. And it would help if there's water.

Does it have to be flat?

No reason.

I just said that because of what I been using it for.

And what is that?

A runway. Landing strip. I been building experimental ultralight planes.

You don't say.

And I might be lookin' to sell out.

How much land you got?

Twelve hundred forty-six acres.

You run any animals on it?

No, but they did before me. I've never grown a thing, just made stuff. So it just is what it is, getting moreso by the minute.

And with that we were off to the races. Once he set his mind to something, Bernie was a go-getter. We named a time to meet at the end of the day, to go have a look at his place. When I swung back around six, the barber pole was turned off, the shades drawn, and he was at the curb, sitting on his bike. He waved at me to follow him out of town to the south. It had been a balmy spring day, and he was riding a Harley Duoglide, with a black helmet and matching leather jacket. I had never suspected. He knew me for a cowboy, with the hat and boots and all, but he also knew I'd been to war. And so had he. It shaped what we talked about, and how we got along. The first haircut he gave me was fine, and I'd tipped him a buck and said I don't care where you learned to work scissors--you got it right. He'd been in the Navy in World War II, aboard a jeep carrier island-hopping in the Pacific. Said he'd gone in the Navy to get as far from Missoura as he could. When I said What'd you do, he said Aircraft mechanic, but mostly got in trouble with authority. Seemed like I spent half the war in the brig. The day he'd told me that, he'd said, Look around this place. You ever wonder who runs a shop with one chair? A loner who gets into it with the boss, who needs it all his own way—that's who. Then he caught himself in the mirror and laughed, and I couldn't help but laugh too.

Near an hour out in the country just past a crossroads we pulled in at a long gravel drive. He ran the bike straight into the barn and shut it off. I pulled to one side of the barnyard, turned around and parked my old pickup off in the weeds. As I got out he walked up, said he needed to talk to his wife a minute, then we'd look around. I said I'd wait right there.

His wife Annalee turned out to be a character all her own, jovial but sharp and bright as brass tacks. Not a thing got by her. She came along for the tour, straight out the kitchen door behind Bernie, wiping her hands on her apron, her long silver hair in a bun with a pair of chopsticks stuck through it. She was one of those who made sure she got in her half of the talkin', so Bernie wouldn't miss explaining anything. I'd got to likin' his stories, and could pretty much see how things stood anyhow. And they were both friendly and direct. If this was a competition to pour my ear full, I didn't mind in the slightest.

The first surprise came in the old barn, which had a huge raised level floor and steel beams that spanned its forty foot width without posts. And on that floor were parked three small bright prop planes. Single-seaters— red, yellow, and blue. A look around told me all I needed to know. With his jigs and jacks, saws and clamps he really had built them right here. Did they all fly? You bet. He showed me stickers and registrations, pulled out a porfolio of color blow-ups of him in the air wearing goggles, even unrolled a set of plans. I asked him Which one flew the best. Bernie said Depends on your needs. The red one—the first one—is still fastest, but is a little squirrelly in much air. Likely needs a bigger tail. The yellow biplane has such a low stall speed you can hover forever, and is the cheapest to fly. But the blue one with the big wheels—the last one— has nice manners, does everything about right, and is the one I'd trust to take me anywhere. A little more comfortable and roomy than the others, with a closed-in cockpit so you don't die of frostbite. I built it back when I was thinking to fly to Alaska. Land on the roads if I had to.

I climbed the staircase to the hayloft, which was roomy but empty. From painted markings on the floor and some jigs it looked like up here was where he had laid out the wings. Then we walked out into the open and looked the land over. There was a creek that wandered down through the place, and a fence around the outside that needed serious work, plus a few gates that were falling apart. I asked if the creek went dry in summer, and Bernie said Not usually. He said they had a good well up by the house, that he'd been told was drilled to eight hundred foot, that never did go dry. It turned out his airstrip was the flattest land on the place, that had been planted to cotton when he first saw it, but had never grown anything since then but weeds. He only kept a long narrow strip mowed to take off and land on. The one decoration they had was a faded orange cone made of cloth, up on a pole, that swiveled to tell which way the wind blew, that Annalee said she had sewn.

When they were done showing me around, I asked if I could see the house and taste the well water, which turned out to have no silt or bite to it, and no odor, that I reckoned the livestock would like. Then Annalee asked if I'd care to stay to supper, which was smelling pretty good—a baked chicken with vegetables, mashed potatoes and gravy. So we washed up and ate, and I thought of a thing or two more to ask, like whether either the barn or the house roof leaked.

Bernie said No, thank goodness—since they're both too steep for my taste.

While we ate Bernie asked me to remind them again what I did in Vietnam. I told them I was what they called a "lurp," a Ranger who went out on those Long-Range Reconnaissance Patrols, a couple for as much as two weeks, hiding in ambush along the main trail down from the north. We were all volunteers, mostly country boys not ascared of the dark or of critters abroad in the jungle. But that didn't mean we're all fearless. When the choppers dropped us off, the downdraft would flatten the tall grass, and we'd feel naked as babies, and run for the nearest jungle, even if it was all lit up shooting at us. The job was pretty simple, once we found the trail north. A dozen or more of us would be strung out in the weeds fifty feet off the trail in a big canoe shape with a light machinegun at the point of either end, with a few Claymore mines on trip wire set out to give us a little early warning. The North Vietnamese mostly ran the trail in the dark, sometimes wheeling their supplies strapped onto bicycles, so we napped in the daylight and ate our MRE meals that mostly tasted like cold canned spaghetti, then at night lay there awake, set for action. The sergeant wouldn't let anyone smoke on patrol 'cause the Cong didn't smoke so could smell it. For the same reason we never had a campfire, which I missed. Usually took me three-four nights till I could fall asleep, and commence to dream I heard horses pounding down the trail. Still get those old nightmares once in a while, that wake me thinkin' I musta done somethin' right, 'cause I'm gettin' a ride outa here, 'cause I'm the only one around who could catch a horse an' ride bareback. But then I always sit up shakin' my head, thinking There's no horses here, they're too good for this dangerous place.

On patrol those runners never did trip a Claymore. They were always a couple sandal-steps ahead of us. Our outfit did manage to pull a few surprises out on patrol, and got a rep as go-getters. But then one night they snuck up in the dark on the far side of the trail and lit us up, come on so strong they just about shot us to pieces, and drove what was left of us out of there.

Bernie said Did you get hurt? I said I got nicked around the edges, but thanks to dumb luck it was nothin' serious. They patched me right up, give me a Purple Heart and sent me back out on patrol. But it was never the same. The fears would get to me sometimes, come and go in waves. What the old-timers called the heebie-jeebies. I'd be down with the fever an' shakes a while, then be fine again. Felt about like the malaria a lot of us caught.

After dinner I helped Annalee and Bernie clean up the dishes, insisted, and that was pretty much it. Took a couple months to get the paperwork straight. The economy was in a slump at the time, so Bernie and Annalee had no other takers anyhow, and the price of land had got soft. They had bought the place for twenty-nine dollars an acre twenty-eight years before, and said they'd take thirty-six cash today. I didn't haggle for a minute, went straight to the bank and the VA, showed them I had two paying jobs and a healthy down-payment, and knew me some tricks raising cattle.

With the papers signed, I started to work on the fence every weekend, patching and setting out some new posts where the old ones had rotted. Once the fence was done I hung some new gates, then moved my good horse Hazel out to the place, along with half a dozen likely-looking heifers I'd bought on time from the family, and while I was at it bred them to their best bull. Took till the second year to fatten their calves up enough to pay the family off, but what the hell, it was a start, and suited me down to the ground. I started calling it the Pipestone, 'cause that was the name of the creek, and it pretty much stuck.

Meanwhile Bernie and Annalee moved into town once they'd sold off those three little planes. They had a little more trouble selling the one-chair barbershop that Bernie said was like selling a one-legged man a pogo stick, easy to take off but tricky landing, but they finally did, when he found someone that hated bosses about as much as he did. Meanwhile he quit charging me for haircuts until they left town the following spring on the Harley, towing a little two-wheeled trailer, headed slow and easy on the back roads back to Missoura, far from the ocean, where he was gonna see if he still belonged, if he could stand the rain back there, that he never quit calling the moisture.

Fixin' to Settle Down

Wouldn't you know it, right in the middle of all that fixing and
building on my new place, somehow tryin' to make the Pipestone a paying
proposition, out of the blue I met someone, and all the puzzle pieces that
hadn't made sense started to drop into place with not much more than a
love-tap. I think that's how you tell if you're on the right track, when all
at once the hard things start gettin' easy, and the easy things just kinda
sort themselves out. You can get awful tired of workin' on your lonesome,
protecting and defending yourself, tired of treating folks around you like
the strangers they'd rather not be, while you shut yourself off, thinking your
own silly thoughts. When you feel yourself open like a plant to the sun after
a long hard winter, it's worth takin' a look around to see what shined on
you, that maybe shook you awake.

And there she was, Muncie Hays, the pretty brandnew meter-read-
er come around for the Rural Electric. She made the outfit look good, in a
green and gold vest and a green hard hat with a gold lightning bolt down
the front, with dark curly hair to her shoulders. She looked all set to jot the
meter numbers down on her clipboard, but said she didn't know where the
meter was, so knocked on my front door to ask. Rebel had barked, jumped
up and went for the door, but quit barkin' right away since she was already
talkin' to him, and he musta liked what he heard. I had been makin' myself
a little lunch, but went and told her I thought it was inside the barn door to
the right, but might be on the outside come to think of it, so I better come
along if she'd wait a second and make sure. I said To tell you the truth I've
never looked at the thing, and might have to wipe away the dust so you can
do your job. I turned off the burner under my grilled cheese sandwich, set
the skillet aside, then showed her the way out the kitchen door and up the

hill to the barn. Rebel tagged right along. I brought along a rag and sure enough needed to spit and scrub to get through the grime to where the little wheels in a row were creeping round. The meter was outside the barn, on the shady side this time of day. She said she had a flashlight in her car, but I'd said Don't bother, I got a flashlight sitting right next to the fusebox inside, and went and got it.

While she was working over her clipboard, I saw the name tag on her vest and said Do you mind me askin' what kind of a name is Muncie? She held up a finger without looking up, wrote down the last number, then said, Sorry, I can't do but one thing at a time. I need to keep the mess-ups to a minimum if I want to keep this job. Always a good thought, I said. She looked me in the eye, smiled and said What was that you were wondering? I said Your name, and pointed to her chest. Oh, she said, that's where my mother's from, upstate Indiana. Where I was born. Nice enough little place with some industry and farming, used to be real busy when the railroads first came through, though since then it's died down.

What do they mostly do there?

I'm not sure anymore. But used to be they made all manner of glass jars and bottles, and cast-iron auto parts. That's where the Ball Brothers built their glassworks, after natural gas was discovered. Gave money to set up Ball State University there. My mother says when she was a girl they had a whole row of foundries blazing round the clock.

What does Muncie mean?

It's a Lenape or Delaware word, the name of the town first settled by the Delaware people in the 1790s. They'd been moved west by the Army, out of New Jersey and Delaware, then got moved again in the 1820s, on west to the far side of the Mississippi, to what would turn out to be Iowa. The white settlers who bought the land from them liked the name of Muncietown but after a while they shortened it down to Muncie. My mom liked it anyhow, said it just meant a belonger, someone who's part of the tribe.

I said I liked it too. Then figured to come right out and said So Muncie, would you care to take a little lunch with me? To which she nodded and flashed that grin, lifted her hard hat and shook out her hair for the first time in that way she always had, that caught the sun.

So we went back to the kitchen. I made her a grilled cheese sandwich to go with mine, and opened some cans of tomato soup to warm in a pan. We talked about a little of everything, slow and easy. After lunch we walked a little ways down Pipestone Creek to look around. She asked if I'd ever found any pipestone here, and I showed her a blue-gray chunk I had back in the barn. She said I thought it was red, and I said only up around the Yellowstone in Wyoming and Montana. This is the same stuff, not quite so pretty, but carves just as easy and smokes just as good.

She liked my cow dog, Rebel, and she liked the only horse I had then, which was Hazel, who was the best. I know now the only reason I ever got anywhere near Muncie was because she got Hazel. That mare was kind to me, and always behaved, but she really listened to Muncie. Hell, she adored her. Pretty much quit following me, took to following her around instead. That's how it is with a good horse, you treat 'em right they get attached, and you can't hardly blame 'em. Somebody really watches and listens to you, gives you their heart, what else you gonna do but return the favor?

And while we looked around we talked some more. Turned out Muncie's name on the birth certificate was really Marybeth, but her parents had moved west to Colorado to follow her dad's job with the Ball Company when she was three, and they just started calling her Muncie as kind of a reminder, since they missed all the friends they'd had back there. When I asked if they ever went back, she looked me in the eye and said You know the answer to that one. I said Yeah, I s'pose I do. She was still formal, and a little wary, but never quit smiling. But then I asked her So how did you wind up in Texas?

Not sure I'm old enough to have wound up anywhere yet. But you know, it's the story of the country, to go see what's over the hill, always turned west to see what the weather will bring. I said That makes good sense. And smiled back. And all at once we were on the other side of whatever the hitch might have been.

And our lunch felt like a good start. She went on back to work, still smiling, and I went back to what I'd been doing, fencing in a garden patch near enough to the well that I could run a hose and pump water. I'd lost my first garden to the deer the year before. I'd let Rebel out the kitchen door to run 'em off in the night, but that was a silly game. Pretty soon he'd get tired and scratch at the door, and they'd come bounding back. Now I was set to get serious. An eight-foot fence should about do it. Once that was up I could line out some rows and start pokin' seed in the ground.

The next day was a Saturday, and I'll be damned if Muncie wasn't knocking on my door right when I'm set to pour coffee. From his patch of sunlight Rebel gave a couple little huffs, but didn't bother barkin'. I realized later he prob'ly already knew the score. She said she'd come to lend a hand plantin' the garden. I grinned, said Sounds like a plan, come on in, then asked if she was feelin' peckish. I fried up some bacon and made a couple stacks of pancakes. When we'd finished that I snatched up the calendar to check the phases of the moon, then we went out and hung the tall gate to close in the fence, then got to layin' out where all the vegetables went, with a few lath sticks and a ball of string. I told her the calendar said it was a waxing moon, so we'd plant all the crops that grew above-ground like tomatoes and peppers and berries, beans and peas, corn and squash, then wait ten days or so for the waning moon to put in the root crops--radishes, potatoes, carrots, onions and beets and the like.

And that's how it went. Without much fanfare we waltzed right through the summer, canned what we couldn't eat fresh, and soon got thicker 'n thieves. We got married in September, and drove to New Orleans for a honeymoon, since neither of us had ever been there. Our first morning there we took a buggy ride all over, behind a big gray mule wearin' a fine straw hat with her ears pokin' through it. Once we got our bearings we mostly walked the cobbled streets of the French Quarter, ate some fancy foods, danced to cajun music and dixieland jazz and slept late. We both loved how it all felt, old and lived-in yet welcoming, breezy and sunny-side-up.

Muncie kept her Rural Electric job for ten years, and seemed to get the neighbors involved in practically everything we did around the place. It was only when they were set to promote her to a desk job overseeing all the meter readers in the county that she balked, since she'd enjoyed going around and seeing all the country folks, how they lived and what they did.

So she took early retirement.

In our life together there seemed to be only one hitch. We couldn't seem to have kids. Which wasn't for lack of trying. But we had a doctor check us both out, and she said we had some fertility issues. Turned out each of us had a little something wrong. But we stopped her right there, asked if it was fixable, and she said likely not. So we left it at that.

And didn't mope. Fact of the matter is, the years flew by. Along in there Rebel slowed to a crawl, stood in the pasture barking orders at the cows, and finally quit helping me herd 'em altogether. Then one hot day while watching me replace some rotten planks in a box stall in the barn, he dozed off and just never woke up. Which may be how it's s'posed to be. Everyday life in all its glory mostly consumed us a little at a time, but left us plenty to laugh at, and meanwhile did us no wrong. Until one day Muncie complained of a little tiredness, trouble catching her breath, and we went in for a checkup. The word that came back was a leaky heart valve. But out in the hallway where she couldn't overhear, her regular doctor told me the specialists had said her heart was junk. Count on country folk not to sugarcoat a road apple.

To my simple way of thinkin' I figured maybe the doctors just hadn't listened so close to her heart because they thought they could see it on the outside plain as day, in what she said and did. But they seemed stricken, stood stiff and felt guilty as I did not noticing. The surgeon told me later they'd thought she had a fair chance, but really should have put her on the list for a heart transplant, and meanwhile just let her lie quiet, since her old ticker was barely holding on. But the list for new hearts was way too long anyhow. They scheduled a surgery, that turned out was already too late. She died on the table, with them working over her.

And that was it. For a while then the lights went outa me, and the air and the rest. I just didn't sleep, lay there staring at the ceiling, couldn't seem to get it straight that she was gone. Spent those nights in the old bed reachin' out my arm across that cold empty place, fingering the far edge. I tried to sleep but could still smell her in the bed with me. After a week or so I scared myself, drifted off and opened my eyes one morning looking around for her smell, and realized I could only smell my own tired, sweaty self. So I stripped the sheets and pillow cases from the bed, washed a load, then hung it out on the line behind the house. When the sheets had billowed dry in the afternoon breeze, I folded and put them away. Then I got out my old Army sleeping bag, and laid it on the bed, and slept soundly for the first night since she'd died.

I slept like that, like a monk in his cell, for a month or two, till I got tired of how bad I was stuck. It was time to move along, and quit kidding myself that Muncie might walk in again any minute. The horses seemed to be looking for her too, wondering what was the matter, watching and listening. Even the calves would stand and stare through me. So that morning I put the sleeping bag in the wash and saddled a good young horse for a long ride in the open to think things out. I brought a canteen and saddlebag of snacks for the horse, apples and carrots, and figured we'd make do with that.

Then late in the day, weaving in and out of deep shadows in a stand of big sagebrush on some state open range land a ways south I remembered how the sarge on those "lurp" patrols in the highlands would tell us, you gotta look out for each other, but you also gotta know what's going on around you, and always look out for yourself. Otherwise you're just killing time, expecting the one with your name on it, maybe secretly beggin' to get it over with.

Which was me to a T. Good thing on the ride home we had apples and carrots to share, 'cause all at once I felt hungry. From then on I was at least awake because at least I slept, and tried to think what to do next. I never did drink myself silly, or much go out in public, or break down an' wreck things. I just stayed home on the place and did my work, just as I had for those eighteen years, like she might think twice about death and double back. Maybe catch me nappin'. But it was a forlorn hope, and at least now I could start to tell myself that. For a while livin' without Muncie had felt like tryin' to talk while chewin' a mouthful a mush, makin' the purest kinda nonsense. Seemed like it took forever to poke myself awake and see how a body can't get by on roughage, without a bite a life, and a little splash of juice to slosh around an' loosen things up.

Goodbye to Haze

That old mare held a story I'd never told a soul, since what you own deeply owns you, makes you that much more yourself. Separate, shaped by a blacksmith's hammer marks that even under the rust of time couldn't be anything else but a glowering hot thing once struck all over to even out the stress, made the hard way what it was, then chilled to stand what was done.

So maybe it was just the flu I couldn't seem to shake, that made everything seem shimmery and vague, that sunk me into that damp bed like I was stuck somewhere in a swamp up to the axles. It was the first time I'd really been sick since my sweet wife Muncie passed on. At the moment I was stumbling around the kitchen fixing myself a little guilty medicine, a toddy of hot lemonade with honey and brown liquor, allowing as how I couldn't feel any worse. It was what Muncie used to fix me for a little pick-me-up when I was ailing, that these days I had to make do for myself. But while stirring my cup I happened to look out the kitchen window at the eight horses in my hillside pasture and there was something wrong. In my weakened and daffy condition at first I thought I'd miscounted. But when I checked again I could see one was down, and another one was bent over close to its head, another half-turned a few steps away on the side of the hill, watching and listening, but trying to ignore what was really going on. The other five horses were bunched up a few lengths away upwind, their tails turned to the horse on the ground, pretending to graze while that one kept watch, head back over one shoulder, body poised to break into a run.

For a beat or two I couldn't recall even which horse it had to be. My hand snatched up the phone but then I looked at it. The dial tone was an accusation, since who was there to call but myself. I set it back down next to my hot cup, and went to the door. There I kicked off my slippers and stepped into my boots. Snatched a quilted plaid shirt off a hook and my stained old gray work hat next to it, then stepped out in the damp chilly air.

It was Hazel, at 34 this spring the oldest horse on the place. The horse nosing closest to her was her granddaughter Harmony. Haze was a dusty dun with black feet, yellow-brown eyes and a face now mottled gray. It was that dark face with the light eyes that first caught at me, that made her seem a little distant and spooky though that wasn't her in the slightest. She was the first horse I'd ever paid cash money for, and had the papers on, but also likely the first who seemed to care a thing for me. I'd grown up in a world where horses belonged to the place, about like the cow hands did, so it was something new when this filly started to follow me around and study my every move. The first day right off she had trusted me. I thought it might be that she'd been weaned too early, had been put up for auction by some penniless fool, entirely too green to be out on her own. Which I was too young to admit had caught at something in me. But with half a year's pay in my pocket, I'd taken a chance on this skinny little filly, and won her at auction while no one with a brain but me had their eyes open. Late that day I'd led her home along the shoulder of the highway, eight miles on foot, since I'd of had to borrow a pickup and trailer nobody seemed willing to lend me. But it was a quiet afternoon without much traffic, and we took the time to get acquainted. I talked and sang tunes to her all the way, like I was just a big kid myself. Which for a fact is mostly what I still was, despite having gone off to war and got shot at and shelled a bunch and come home with kind of a rind on me, a rough bark. By the time we got to the front gate and turned into the yard she was halfway set to tote me wherever I wanted. Next morning I named her for those yellow-brown eyes, and for a favorite maiden aunt of mine who'd taught third grade and was pure magic with the kids. From then on I mostly took my cues from her, and what I didn't notice in time she mostly forgave.

Before Hazel I had broken horses the old way, climbed aboard and rode the fight out of them till they were done bucking. But then I went to Vietnam late in the war, got shot at and ducked, serving what they called my tour of duty. The army showed me I didn't have much choice in the matter, and one night in my bunk I found myself recalling the horses back on the home place, how they never had much choice either. Here up in the provinces along the Ho Chi Minh Trail you had a good excuse to play crazy, what with the tunnels and bombing runs and Agent Orange, which mostly meant the sergeant would ride the fight out of you till you gave. Or else a doctor having a bad day might just sign your papers and wreck his own chances at the good life somewhere back stateside. On the home place I'd heard the occasional hand say there was a better way to work horses, but I'd never seen it done, from my grandfather nor father either one, nor any of the hands they hired and rode herd on, till I was up and away on my own.

By now I hadn't ridden Haze in a dozen years, yet she'd still lift her head and nicker at me every other time I came out the kitchen door headed for the barn. She was the only horse that had never fought me for a minute, let me have my way and gave me her wholehearted best. Still we'd both been young and she'd been worked hard, sorry to say, and started to lose her footing earlier than some other horses we had. There would always be too much work for those like Haze that are willing and able, with that peculiar aptitude working cows. But that also meant she'd earned her retirement fair and square, and nobody was going to take it away from her. On the Moon-Dog spread I'd known a fancy old parade horse or two that never got wore down, hardly even got dirty, and seemed not to mind getting gussied up for the stroll down Main Street the 4th of July. My grandpa and father favored palominos with long bright manes and tails that swept the ground. But I was never much for parades or fancy rigs, kept the uniform in a closet, and would just as soon spend the holiday on the porch in the shade, with an iced tea or cold beer nearby and the radio on.

Now here she lay on the hillside, her last legs out from under her. As I stepped close and bent down, she huffed and nickered at me, a hollow miniature of her old song. I sat down, lifted her head and slid myself under. And rubbed her neck and talked to her. I said it would be fine, she could still kick up her heels and run in her dreams like the wind. I remembered it was Haze who'd taught me how to get along with horses, to be clear and steady and in no hurry, talk friendly and watch for signs she was ready to take the next step. So what else could I do—I stroked her shoulder and thanked her.

After a little while setting there I started slapping my shirt pockets, a reflex looking for a treat, but then I found a little something, a strawberry gummy bear covered with lint that I sat there and tried to pick off. This is how it had always been with Haze—a little something new every day. A little puzzle to unwrap like a piece of candy—a taste, a smell, apple or slice of raw beet or a pink square of bubblegum. Something in the hand I would hold out and offer her. I'd had her every day for all those twenty-something working years, then beyond, and nearly always had something, shoulda made a list of what it was she liked, just one a day.

So I slipped that hard sweet fuzzy little thing in the corner of her mouth, and she took it and worked it around with her tongue. Not much comfort, that stale thing rattling against her teeth for what seemed like the hours it became. Haze didn't gather herself, or flail about, or even try to get up. If she had I'd a helped lift and encourage her. But there was more of her down than both of us could handle, so we sat quiet like that, going downhill, with all the other horses still a little fearful and stand-offish, near as they dared, until with a long rattling sigh she went, and I let her go with both my stiff old hands still holding on. Then I lifted her heavy head up offa me, slid out from under and went back into the kitchen to drink my cold medicine and change into some dry clothes, and think about digging a hole. But first I laid down on that damp empty bed, shivered and shook a little for the living that never quits for a minute, that lets go before you've even planted your feet and got set for the ride alone in the dark that's to come.

Mud Puppies

After Muncie died things were slow getting back to normal--and normal itself seemed to change. First, my grandfather died, to a thunderous silence. He'd been 95, had known and done it all, and what was there to say? But then within a couple years a drought snuck up when I wasn't looking, that stretched on and on, five years in all, that seemed worse than anything I'd seen. Not that we didn't have dry spells when we were kids. We'd get what I was told mama used to call a little "homemade weather." Thin patches of rain all torn up and scattered round. Then they said sometimes she'd call it a "tester," as in "The Lord's just testing us," point up at high puffy clouds that might slow just long enough to squeeze out a few drops, to settle the dust in the road. Great round drops that would splat and each raise a cloud like a miniature crown, that would streak down our dusty faces, leave a shiny faint track like a snail. But that would be it, no real rain for the deep baked-in cracks in the dirt, for the pale rattling cornstalks with scarce a snuff tin's worth of kernels to the cob, for the grass with no green and no life left.

But this time it got worse. Calves, their heads hung low, bawling in any shade they could find, water troughs with dead birds floating in them, that would swoop and hover trying to catch a drink, fall in and drown. Got so we'd float a dead tree branch in each of the metal troughs we used to water stock, so a swallow, swift or sparrow might climb out and dry off enough to save itself. We fed all the grain, beans and corn we had, all the hay too, then bought hay at double then triple the price till there was none to be had at any price for five states around.

Finally that Pipestone Creek that ran down through the big pasture, that we'd taken to calling Little Trickle, dried up to where the banks gave just enough shade for a couple damp spots in the bed, that held a few horned toads and lizards set to blink at whatever passing looked down. By the third summer even our one deep well tasted muddy. Finally there was nothin' for it but to thin the herd, down to the runts, the stunted nubbins. Along in there I had to lay off the two cowhands I'd had forever, Reynaldo and Clyde, with nothing much left for 'em to do, nor what-for to pay 'em with. I told them they could stay for free in the bunkhouse, and share in the garden we'd always planted and watered past sundown, but would have to fend for themselves otherwise till things looked up. We even rigged shade canvas for some of the garden on top of the tall deer fence, to grow greens and berries under, with a mulch of rotten straw bedding from the barn knee-deep in spots to hold the moisture.

That was when every trick got tried, every hope that still lay in good breeding stock, or what some had mixed in with hardy old longhorns and mustangs. I'd found a young doe dead in the far pasture, that had a mouthful of cactus spines stuck so tight she'd starved to death. The next night I went out with a lantern and cut a wagonload of that same cactus, then singed all the stickers off next morning with a blowtorch, careful not to miss a one. I hacked it all up with a machete to feed the heifers, those few of the best I had left. The cattle actually ate it, though it was a feed the skinny horses still wouldn't touch. That was when ranchers and farmers started going out after dark, mowing and baling the median and shoulders along the freeways. It was a desperate move, but everybody knew by now it was that or nothin'. The state troopers and deputy sheriffs showed up, but just waved the traffic around us, let us be, shared our coffee and like the old song goes, never said a mumbling word.

Along in there one morning I was sitting in the shade in the open mouth of the barn, cleaning and oiling the saddle I hadn't used in months, with only those two good mares left, studying some mud daubers huddled around a splash of water under the nearby well spigot. I'd always liked these skinny black wasps that seemed a little sleepy but deliberate, tickin' and twitchin' like each was an old windup clock. They were mostly loners forever busy and quiet, never offered to sting me or bother anything. But this morning they seemed a little fired up, in more of a hurry to mix the mud and get to layin' their eggs and catchin' a spider or moth to wall in with the baby-to-be. Most of these little mamas were totin' balls of mud up under the eaves of the barn overhead, building their parallel tubes in the joints where the roof planks met the wall. They usually did good work, and I usually admired how they did it, but today saw they had mostly quit, and were back down checking the spigot. The puddle was drying up. The air was so hot and dry the mud would crumble and crack before they could even smooth it out. And what could they do about that? Some predator might find a crack and get in. Their eggs might cook and never hatch. So I set the saddle aside, went over and ran the spigot enough to make 'em a serious puddle six feet across, and wired an old umbrella up over it. Which stopped me and them mud daubers mopin' a minute, and got us all back to work.

For a while there I wasn't sure that any of it would come back. But I'd bought some grass seed and wildflower seed and red clover just in case, maybe to have something to do the day after the rains come, or something to feed the birds in case they never did. In my heart I just got down in the dirt with the rest of 'em, figured we'd all take our chances the same.

One night rockin' on the porch the answer come to me that I should plant some trees. I had plenty of land with nothin' much growing on it. So I got out the books and catalogues to see what might do best, then bought a notebook and got a list going. Every late winter for three of those five years I'd buy a couple or three of some kind of tree that could stand the heat, and wasn't too thirsty, so made sense. I hung out at the nursery the next town over, and picked the folks' brains clean down to the collar-bone. I figured to need some shade along the creek, so planted a clump of live oak trees around one damp spot, and a batch of burr oaks around the other spot, and put up an eight foot fence around each clump, so the cattle and deer couldn't eat 'em to nothing before they shot up out of reach, got their growth and started to fend for themselves.

Over time rockin', sittin' quiet on the porch I came up with the start of a plan. The first note I wrote in that spiral notebook after trees was cisterns, printed at the top of a page in big letters, with my thinking gathered underneath. Something to catch the runoff from the barn and house, a couple big concrete boxes underground where the rain could be stored, that wouldn't evaporate so fast. I knew it meant a lot of work, and most old houses and barns in the country never had gutters anyhow. But from now on we'd need to save every drop. I had to get a couple tall ladders, and plywood for forms, then sketch out and figure the measurements. That would be the hard part--how much water did we need? I found in a book on cattle-raising that a full-grown cow needed roughly 10-20 gallons of water a day, 10 in winter and 20 in summer, and a third more if she was nursing a calf, or was a calf in her first year's growth spurt, so 30 gallons. A horse would need 10-12 gallons a day depending on the weather and how hard it was working. That meant each cow would need roughly 5500 gallons a year, 7300 gallons if a mother cow or a growing calf its first year, and a horse would need 3600 to 4000 gallons a year, depending how hard it was worked and how hot it got. Soon I was thinkin' a good start would be a year's worth of water on tap, for every cow and horse and human on the place, and more if we could get it. I finally decided even Pipestone Creek might be gathered into a cistern of its own, kept cool and wet underground not far from the barn, that could be pumped up in moments of need. While studying water I even dug a hole and slapped together an outhouse that might take me decades to fill.

On the next page I wrote crops, and on the page after that green-house. There might be things we could grow that didn't take so much water, that weren't so easily beaten down by the sun. Something even picky horses might still eat. Like oats and winter wheat. And I started to see we'd have to make use of whatever shade we had till there were trees.

But for the last couple years of the drought we hadn't stirred the dirt, or planted a thing in the fields, and there was nothing standing up for itself out there but a smattering of weeds. Then, when everyone had about given up twice over, out of what looked like a clear but faded blue sky the rains came. And when the rains came they came hard--it rained a year's worth in half an hour, and that went on for weeks. As with most of the cowhands around here, that first day I just stood out in the rain whoopin' and hollerin', gettin' soaked to the skin. Renaldo and Clyde came out of the bunkhouse laughin', with me or at me I didn't care, and we cut a little buck and wing skippin' around in the puddles. Before I got back to the house, my old everyday boots had about fell apart. My soles would need to be glued and stitched back together. But I wasn't likely to forget, and got busy storing up what I could, and preparing for the next dry spell that might start up any minute.

But these rains and storms didn't just ease in, they slam-banged and knocked everything flat. They had soaked everyone and everything that ran outdoors to be blessed. The roofs of barns and houses, gas stations, churches and feed stores all leaked--all their shingles and seams in the heat had long ago shriveled and split. The hardware store had no buckets for customers; they'd had to set out every brand new bucket in stock to mind their own dribbles.

So it took a while to mop up. But after a few weeks it was like the drought had never been. A five-year drought that had mostly been a stretch of nothing but heartache. In the flinty, cracked hardpan no crops would take, none at all, no matter how fine we harrowed it. Got so we never made a move if there was any wind atall, that would just lift up and blow off what was left of the dirt. For that last two summers we didn't stir or plant a thing, left the weedy hardpan alone.

While I was taking stock, wondering where to begin and what was my next move, out of the blue my dad called. We didn't see each other much anymore but for his birthday, Thanksgiving and Christmas. But he needed to run into the city for a doctor's appointment, and wondered if I'd care to drive, then go to the racetrack with him. It was something we'd done a few times when I was a kid, that and rodeos, and had always had a good time--but I hadn't been to the track since I got out of the service. His plan was we'd drive up the day before, stay at a motel, and have us a good dinner somewhere. His appointment was next morning, and he'd checked, and the racetrack opened at one. I figured maybe he just wanted a chance to talk with nobody else much around.

Over lunch at a little barbecue place Dad asked Did you ever think it would get this bad?

I said What do you mean exactly? He said You know, the heat, the drought, brush fires and the like. I figured we probably wouldn't have much to talk about, since he already knew what I thought of his oil deal, and the oil business itself--the fossil fuels and fracking and the rest, that had about finished off his big ranch as a paying enterprise. But he'd wanted me to come along not just to play chauffeur. And the old man finally opened up about always doing what his father, my grandfather, wanted. And when it came down to the oil, he'd known it was just how money talked tough to old age, nothing else. Making it all sound so easy, just sit back and cash the checks. And now, with the old man gone to his reward just after Muncie had, he was asking what I thought. I told him I thought we were really in for it. This climate change was real, and world-wide, and would make it hard to raise cows, or do much of anything sensible with summers all sun and no rain, with range fires on the loose. It was gonna take a lot more than luck to get through, and no mistake.

He took it different than he ever had before, more level an' quiet. He didn't just jump in with both feet like he used to, mocking and badgering to shut me up. I could tell he'd been mostly just performing for his father, playing the loyal lieutenant, backing the old man's play to the hilt. He said What do you figure to do, and I told him a little about the plans I was working on, to dig, frame up and pour cement for some cisterns, and a tornado shelter while I was at it, since that was another kind of disaster that was only gettin' worse. Then hang some gutters and downspouts, and all along plant some good trees. Maybe put up a sturdy greenhouse and a wind generator, try to grow some different things. I went on and on with all the stuff in that notebook I'd gathered up, that I'd been lookin' for, pricing and plannin' on. Like always he was lookin' hard at me, but for once sat still, nodded and listened.

When we got to the track Dad was still kinda worked up, but still not sayin' much. The sky had gotten dark, like it was fixin' to bust a good 'un. Then in the first race of the day, with the horses halfway around the track on the far stretch, it cut loose, rumblin' and flashin' a couple good licks, then the sky opened up and down it came. We were in covered seats under a leaky roof ourselves, and all at once we're soaked to the skin and both laughing. Most horses at the track look fancy and fussy, in all their colors and rigs. Jockeys dressed head to foot in bright silks. But here all at once they were what as a kid I'd called mud puppies. All the same mud color, hard to read their numbers or tell the jockeys' colors, everything a brown movie that swirled and flitted and splashed by in the home stretch--their ears back, noses out, necks stretched, eager and running wide open. Happy mud puppies.

Some horses like to run in the rain and the mud, and some don't. Some are mudders, some aren't. A rain can change the odds on everything. Some are set for it and run strong in the mud--some slip and slide and get cautious, some don't. But today these all looked happy, whether first or last. They'd been through the drought too, took the wet for the blessing it was, and knew what was what. We hadn't even bet on this first race, because we were still fighting the drought, a million miles off in our heads. But then we bought a Racing Form, and for the rest of the day bet all mudders. And the good ones mostly won, as we knew they would. And on the drive back to the motel, after a long silence Dad called me a mudder, a good ol' mud puppy that didn't mind the rain, and if I would just keep on runnin' he said he was bettin' on me.

What Little There is in the Ground

Past the big drought was when I had finally got off the pot, and sold ten of the eleven frontage lots I had along the county road to the east. I'd told myself it was to fund my retirement. Three acres apiece, which was a drop in the bucket—I still had over 1200 acres, a little in hay and beans, but mostly in cattle and calves. I was sick of watching sunrise crawl over that pasture, that made my blinded cattle turn head to the wind, that was bad for them, fogged in as it was some mornings spring and fall. I figured houses there might break the glare and give me something besides the paper over coffee to consider. So it was both by happenstance and consequence out this far that I finally had what amounted to neighbors. In the old days I'd used to run off the few neighbors when they'd came by for the loan of a shovel or garden hose. I'd say Do I look like a hardware store? Get your own damn hose. But then my old cow dog Rebel had died, then in short order my wife Muncie, of a bad heart valve they'd somehow missed, and I lightened up. Muncie had been a good old gal with a sweet sashay about her, how she launched her wide hips and solid self deep into everybody's business, and I missed her sorely. We weren't able to have kids but had shared everything else large and small. Besides, what did a garden hose matter? It was no skin off my nose, as my high school buddy Cosgrove used to say down at the service station before he sold out and moved to Arizona, where he said it was hot as blazes and everything green seemed to bite you then die. So now here I was selling a few patches of land for cheap, and bought cheaper hoses and left them hanging on nails in the shed in their plastic packaging, for when somebody mowing their yard ran over theirs.

Lord knows I was no saint, though for my whole life hereabouts I had resisted the allure of oil. It had always been easy to say no. I just didn't crave that kind of dirty money. I was a cattleman, one of those farming kind who needed hay and oats and corn to feed my livestock through the winter, and water when it got dry. And I did what I needed to get it, mostly by growing my own. I knew good and well how horses didn't mix with oil, how they balked at the smell and feel of it. In the early days of cars there had been stories of people who parked their shiny new contraption in the stall next to their horse, and woke in the morning to find a dead animal. Sometimes with injuries from trying to climb the walls, sometimes dead without a mark. All of which told you something that each had to learn for himself.

The hands who could work on cars said it was the old updraft carburetors, dogleg things with bad gaskets and seals that leaked gas, and they might have been right. These old rutted back roads could sure dismantle an engine while they shook the teeth from your head. Pretty quick it got to be that nobody who cared about a horse would keep it in a shed or garage that had been used to house cars, that all sweated gas and grease and oil and antifreeze right from day one. Even under a foot of bedding or fodder, there were poisons a good horse shouldn't have to stand for, and who didn't know they mostly slept standing.

These days I worked the place singlehanded, but for several times a year trading work with a couple neighbors who were in the same fix. Haying I'd used to get Muncie to drive the tractor that pulled the flatbed wagon, and she could steer a row with the best of 'em while I bucked bales. I used to have a couple hired hands who lived in the bunkhouse I'd built, that cooked for themselves every day but Sundays, and helped me do a little of everything around the place. But no more. I am still ashamed to say I ran out of the what-for to pay them. So at first I hated doing it all by myself, as if I was trying to prove something, if only to Muncie and Rebel. But with them both gone during the recent drought I'd cut back on the herd, when I had to sell off most of the breeding stock, and all but two of our mares. By then it got so I savored the quiet in the fields and barn, that at least let me carry on with what some folks called my loopy old daydreamy ways.

Then one spring morning two small skinny boys wandered across the pasture while I was out digging a hole in the yard. From a distance they seemed to the casual eye like they oughta be twins, though when I studied them one was a little taller and walked half a step ahead while the other skipped to keep up. Crossing the field they dodged the cows, didn't spook or bother them or step in anything, came to stand around the hole and look in, said hi, then overcoming their shyness commenced to ask me all manner of questions about what I was up to—could I really dig clear to China, for example, that seemed obvious till all at once I remembered the kind of kid I had been. So I slowed down, doubled back to introduce myself, gravely shook hands with Ike and Mo Mosley, short for Isaac and Moses, showed them how I kept the black dirt and the yellow dirt in two separate piles, explained why, answered their questions and chatted for hours while the hole got deep and wide enough to spread the roots out and get the tree planted for a long, fruitful life. The two of them held the rooted slip of a peach tree straight while I filled in the hole with topsoil and a sprinkling of compost, then tamped it all gently down, and watered till it wouldn't take another drop.

But from then on word got out. It seemed like all at once these new neighbor kids noticed I had animals, and started feeding the calves and horses handfuls of grass through the fence. Which was fine with me, though I cautioned the kids to stay on their own side of the wire so they wouldn't get stepped on. Cows' and horses' eyesight didn't work the same as ours, and these critters were no way pets.

But then came the oil anyhow. The last of the lots on the far end was bought by a man with two grown sons. I figured all three worked off somewhere in town—little did I know, since they'd paid me cash. Big rough old man Maximillian Donnelly and his two big roughneck boys cut of the same cloth, Whit and Brat. When they poured some footers, then banged up a house in eight days in one corner of the lot, in a big hurry right through the nights with halogen lights, nail guns and compressors, and a boom-box playing Tex-Mex music, right next to the road rather than set back in the middle like all the others going up, I should have known. By the time they moved into the house they already had a drilling rig set up, over the lot's exact center.

And if the neighborhood thought they'd framed and closed in the house in a hurry, that wasn't a patch to how they worked the rig, that soon had the boom-box and lights and drill clanking and banging through the night. It seemed they couldn't wait to get at it, and sleeping neighbors be damned. So I went over and talked to them twice, trying to keep it polite, but then on the third night I called Sheriff Hanrahan, and Larry came out an hour later, pulled in with his roof bar lit up, and put on his specs to study their paperwork. He told the Donnellys to hold down the noise between six at night and seven in the morning. To which Maximillian said You can't expect a man to pussyfoot around an oil rig, but the sheriff stopped him right there, said I am done talking. Clean out your ears. This land is not zoned industrial. You will bygod keep it down. One more complaint, one, and you're gonna talk to Judge Benzinger. And bygod in his woodshed you'll talk nice. So the nightly boom-box and slam-bang stopped, and the clanking quieted as the hole deepened, though the drilling ran on through the summer nights, clear down into fall.

And I saw pretty quick what I could do was nothing much. There were no oil wells hereabouts, for a couple hundred miles. Not all of Texas was an oil patch. But the oil mostly bought and paid for the politics. And the fact was the Donnellys had bought my last lot on the lowest land, and they had the mineral rights, that they'd never said a word about, but down at the courthouse I learned they'd researched and filed on their own little piece and paid the fees, most likely the old man Max who served as both mouth and brains of the outfit.

For a cattleman, I knew more than I cared to about wildcatters and roughnecks. How they'd leave a smelly damn lagoon with no fence around it, a trap for the unwary and innocent, that livestock, especially calves, might wander into, get stuck and then swallowed up. But it was mostly the attitude, how laws didn't matter, so long as they could find the stuff, somehow drill down and pump it out, and how the money always worked to buy you clean. You'd come off a two-week stint on the rig, go get a steam-bath, shave and haircut and new suit of clothes, order a big thick steak dripping blood with a frosty mug alongside, and there you set sassy as a jaybird, and it's like that slippery smelly rig never even was.

Wildcatters hoped to crack the nut and get all the meat for themselves. And why not? They worked rusty jury-rigged equipment, felt like they took all the risk, treated it like gambling, and often as not drilled dry holes. The big boys at Texaco and Sunoco, Atlantic Richfield, Exxon Mobil, Sinclair and the rest had their experts, took their soundings and measurements, so more often struck a gusher. But it was still a smelly, risky business mostly spent sniffing around in the dark a mile or two underground. They'd check the bit once or twice a shift to see what they were cutting through, and tried to keep careful notes—what and where and how deep down, never knowing when or if the stuff might come spouting up.

A wildcatter was always selling some widow or retired old farm couple the dream, with never a word about how it would likely come up empty, this invisible, long-buried promise. Of course he had to make a mess to find out if the black gold was even there. But then if it was, he stood ready to sell the idea of a regular income where you never lifted a finger, pumped up by the barrel as long as it might last. The only downside was the pumpjack, that ugly iron insect thing out in the field with its screeling sound, that went up and down forever round the clock, bothering the animals, trailing a whiff of methane on the wind.

So as the fall went on, I kept hoping what for me might as well have been a miracle, though for them the normal course of business—a dry hole. Their equipment was worn-out, old and slow, and they'd been drilling eighty-four days nonstop when early one morning the ground shook and up it came, splashing and splattering black gold. The Donnellys would have to pay to have the nearest neighbor's new house pressure-washed, when the wind shifted while they were capping it off. But they were laughing as they said they were sorry and would get right on it, called it just the cost of doing business. And of course the oil seeped under my fence onto my land, and I had to get them to help me fence the puddle so my livestock wouldn't get into it before they scraped and hauled it away. Working on the fencing they were still laughing a little as they ran off my cattle and horses, that just wanted to study the fuss. Time we were done I was achin' to give the Donnelly boys a little lesson in manners.

That first few days' yield was pretty light, maybe a dozen barrels a day, but then it picked up. After the second month Maximillian bought himself a new red truck, and a white Mustang convertible for his boys to tear around in. The place by then was a nonstop party with music and dancing, barbecue and kegs, and stray girls with big hair and long nails and short skirts. I had no idea what kinda money that rig might be pumping, but the old man and his boys were doing their damnedest to keep up with it. When they were flush, the Donnellys could be open-handed, so the neighbors along the county road mostly had no complaints. Once they brought in what they called the walkin' bug, which was the pumpjack to pull up the oil, it got almost quiet, and when they threw a party everyone was invited. I finally got to chat with Eva and Clint Mosley, who were the cheery young parents of those two solemn little boys who'd helped me plant that peach that was growing nicely toward yielding a few annual pies. I said I'd noticed the boys weren't around to watch the drilling rig work, and both parents said they'd been warned, and if I saw them over there to shake a stick at 'em and send them home. On second thought, Clint said, forget that stick part. I said I could see they were good boys, but knew what he meant.

Then all at once it was done. The pumpjack was sucking foul-smelling gases and sand.

The Donnellys went around and let the neighbors know they'd be drilling again, then they set up and started the rig and said they'd give it another few weeks. They went down another 800 feet before they called it quits and shut down for good. One near neighbor offered to let them try a hole on his lot if they'd go halves on whatever turned up. Max gave a pained smile and said No thanks, then come over one morning and offered to sell his three acres back to me, asking ten grand for the unpainted house they'd thrown up, saying at that he'd almost break even. Though I couldn't afford it, I bought the place back just to see them gone.

On Maximillian's last day, the wildcatter came up on my porch and pointed across the pasture at where that iron grasshopper was cycling up and down in slow motion. He looked me in the eye and said She's still pumping a dozen barrels a week. I could give you a deal on that pumpjack, that over time would always pay you a little something. I shook my head before the man was done. Said Cap the well and take that damn thing with you. When Max said What about the oil, I said Leave what little there is in the ground.

Halfway down the steps Donnelly turned around, and said Mr. Whittaker—Brick? No hard feelings. I'm a natural-born boomer is all. Follow where the work goes and the lights is bright and the pay's good. I got into wildcatting only because this one old boy practically owed me his life's blood, and the one thing he had worth a dime was that rig. It was that or nothin', so I took it, and it's been up and down, round and round ever since. Guess you could say I got hooked. Never sure what we'll hit or when or how much, but it sure gets your attention when she blows. Then we shook hands in goodbye, my hand hard and calloused as his.

When the Donnellys pulled out at dawn the next morning, all their trailers and gear strung out in a caravan, they left the keys in the mailbox like I'd said. After my morning coffee I went over for a looksee, and wasn't in the least surprised by the mess I found. Starved weasels in a cage could have done no worse chewing through sofas, tin cans and wall board. I shoveled it all out into the yard with my aluminum grain scoop, burned up what would burn and took the rest into town to recycle. Late that afternoon I ground off the threaded rods that had held the pumpjack down to its concrete pad, scrubbed off the oil stain there with powdered laundry soap till it come halfway clean, then got Clint Mosley, the handy father of those big-eyed little boys, to give me a hand moving my big picnic table over to cover that eyesore of a rusty wellhead that no one around here would likely forget exactly where it once stood. But moving that table was a chore, since the oversized homemade thing wouldn't fit in my truck so we had to carry it by hand a good quarter-mile. The deal I made with Clint was that I'd give the boys a riding lesson the first day they were free, which turned out to be next morning early, when I woke to their two stout little knocks on my door.

Pure Hopeless

Time flies no matter if it's fun or a heartache you're having, and it all speeds up with age, till you wonder where the morning went before the first real hunger pang.

My two little neighbor boys turned out to be horsey fools before we'd even worked up an appetite. Ike and Mo were six and five, agile and fearless as cats. Ike was the thoughtful, serious one, always measuring his words and gauging his effect--with a cowlick that stood straight up in back. Mo was a pretty straight shooter too, but with a bit of the joker about him and no cowlick at all. I'd already showed 'em how to feed a horse, pulling their fingers together with the apple or whatever flat on their open palm. It was lucky I had a couple of old saddles with room to punch new holes and shorten the stirrups to fit, and could leave my own saddle alone, that had taken forever to fit me right. But since I only had Lady and Beulah, I spent the morning getting the boys acquainted with the two mares in the big open pasture. When I introduced them, tied up outside the barn in the morning shade at the hitching rail, I asked which horse they thought was older, and they both said Lady since she was dappled gray, while Beulah was a bay, with a black forehead and muzzle, and four black feet and legs that made me recall my first horsey dreamboat, Hazel. So I said Here, let me show you, and opened Lady's mouth and pulled her lips back so they could see her teeth. I explained about cutters and grinders, then pointed to her incisors that were worn pretty level, with a dish in the middle of each tooth that showed she was about eight years old. Then I turned to Beulah and opened her mouth, and the boys could see her incisors were worn a little flatter, with almost no cup to them, so she must be ten if she's a day.

So Mo, you get Lady, and Ike will ride Beulah. When they asked why, I said it likely took an older boy to work an older horse. These horses get smarter by the year, just like some folks that never quit learnin'. I showed them how the saddle went on, and how to feed the straps under and around, and watch how the horse held her breath, and then to wait to cinch it tight till the horse let out all that air. But then I realized I was wastin' my own breath, since the boys weren't strong or tall enough to lift a saddle that high much less cinch it tight, so I had another thought, heaved the saddles back down and dropped them over a pair of sawhorses just inside the barn door. I figured it might be just as well if we practiced leading the horses first. I told them You want to walk a little to one side so the horse can see you good, and won't step on you, since dead-ahead and dead-behind are her blind spots. Then I told them they had to show the horses who was boss. How do you think you do that? You want her to stop when you stop, so you tell her Whoa. You need to convince her you are holding on so tight you'll be like the anchor to her boat. Hold the reins tight but with a little give to your knees and elbows, that'll make the horse have to pick you up off the ground to even turn her head. Then right away Mo said How do I make her go, so we practiced clicking our tongues and saying Giddyup, which got a stare from the horses since no one had taken a step.

I watched the boys pretty close myself, and they were both careful and serious, but it was all brand-new that first day, so I wasn't about to turn 'em loose. For a couple hours we just wandered down the little cattle trail that ran alongside Pipestone Creek and followed it clear south to the end of my land, at that pool right under the old highway bridge. I knew the boys were caught in a blend of daring and fear—they just wanted to climb on and gallop, and here I had them leading horses, which wasn't half as exciting and maybe a little more scary. And here they both were, so small and new, seeing everything up close through the eyes of the horses, also new to them but huge, looming over them. And as soon as they got close to the little stream, the horses wanted a drink. I stopped them all, and said you notice Lady and Beulah pulling you that way? Ike said I figured to let her have a drink anyhow. I said Good, just make sure it's you that

decides when and where. Mo said But I couldn't stop her anyhow. I said Yes
you could. These horses want to get their way, just like people, but they're
also trained to be obedient and polite. 'Cause that's how I raised 'em. All
you have to do is hold on tight and insist. Insist? Both boys looked up at
me. I said What do you say when you want them to stop? Whoa, they both
said the same instant. And both horses stopped perfectly still. And we all
laughed. Then the horses got their drink of water.

The boys were new as wet-paint-on-a-barn new, new as fuzzy baby
birds in a nest all mouth and gobble. I was actually having more fun than
I shoulda, spending the morning out in the big field hobbling along after
them. And saw them get more confident. And saw things I didn't expect.
Like when Ike scooped up a little water in his palm to taste and see was it
worth letting Beulah drink. That coulda been me at that age. Mo even held
out his hand to show Lady a grasshopper he'd caught, that startled them
both as it spread its wings and whirred off. And neither boy let go of those
reins for an instant.

When we got back to the barn I turned the horses into the corral, took their bridles off and let the boys feed 'em a couple flakes of hay. I
explained how they could eat with a bit in their mouth, but was not much
fun since it was in the way, and fit in that gap between their front and back
teeth. And besides, it prob'ly made the hay taste funny. Then I piled Ike and
Mo into the pickup to take them home to their mom, though it wasn't but
a quarter-mile away, and ask if we could maybe get some lunch in town.
By then they were both calling me Mr. Brick, that they must have liked the
sound of better than Whittaker, though it didn't much matter.

We pulled into the Mosleys' gravel yard and I sent them in to talk
to their mom. But by the time Eva Mosley met me at the front door and
invited me in, the boys were already halfway through their chicken-noodle
soup and peanut-butter-and-jelly sandwiches. There was even a plate of the
same for me, with coffee, so I guess we weren't going much of anywhere.

While I stirred and blew on my soup, Eva asked me Did the boys
behave? I looked at them and said They sure made those horses behave, and
they giggled. They called me Mr. Brick in front of their mom, which seemed
to suit her just fine too. So when lunch was done, we went back to my barn

and did one more little project I'd thought of. We dug out some rope and I started measuring and tying knots. Mo asked what I was making, and I said I'm making you some real stirrups. Ike said What do you mean? I said the word stirrup just means a "rup" or rope to climb on a horse with. "Stigen" means to climb. That's what the word meant back before they made the first saddle. Then I made 'em each a "climber" to help 'em get into the saddle. There was a small loop to go over the horn and a big loop to put their foot in at the bottom, then a knot every foot or so on the way up. When we were done I strapped a saddle on top of a tall gate, and let them practice scrambling up. They caught on quick, and both liked this idea of a "climber" just fine. Then I saddled the two mares, and for the rest of that afternoon, I rode Lady while the two of them rode Beulah. I watched the boy in the rear for when he'd get restless, that called for a stop to let them switch seats so the other one got a chance to hold the reins and run the show. The first time we stopped Ike had the reins and Beulah didn't exactly stop. I said Do you boys know who Lincoln was? Mo said He's on the penny. Ike said He's the one who freed the slaves. I said You boys are sharp. Well, Lincoln once asked some Congressmen How many legs does a dog have, if you count his tail as a leg? I studied them a minute. Neither boy made a sound. I told them Lincoln said Four. Counting a tail as a leg don't make it one. You've got to be clear in your mind what you want, then let the horse know so she'll do just that, nothin' else. Don't just let her ease to a stop, tell her Whoa with your voice and your hands. Then every time she does just exactly what you want, reward her with a little attention.

These were good boys, that even when I was funnin' with 'em caught on quick. They really liked how both horses would stand stock-still when their reins hit the ground, what the cowboys called "ground-tied." I told them that was just good for a minute, till they knew the horses better. Any longer and they ought to be held or tied to something solid.

That second morning after the boys knocked again polite but early, we got in the pickup and went down to O'Grady's Stock Barn over on the other side of town, to look over the postings for next Saturday's auction, and scout a new horse for myself. Only half the stalls were occupied, but as we walked along the boys wanted to know what I was looking for, so I got to explain what made a good cow pony. Which wasn't so much looks as attention and attitude. While we were talking all at once I realized that up to this moment I had mostly been setting around getting ready to die, at least acquainted with the notion, keeping things a little too simple and shallow, stalling and kidding myself. I hadn't bothered to ask what I really wanted in years, and all at once here it was, dressed up like a young cow horse, that made me stop and catch my breath. Sure, it was likely a shabby excuse for wanting grandkids, which since Muncie and I had never had kids of our own was pure hopeless. But sometimes a gift comes to you out of the blue, and there was something to this business of passing things on, at least getting these two boys started right, showing them a thing or two about stuff they might want to know anyhow. Besides, a young horse of my own might take up a little of the day-to-day slack, while I taught it to take me around and work cows.

That night sitting around with their parents Clint and Eva, after a long dusty afternoon in the saddle with Ike and Mo, I found myself recalling the days of the recent drought, when farmers and ranchers had mown and baled the median grass and shoulders of the freeways, for something to feed their stock. I'd liked the idea, but there were no freeways nearby, where I could haul my equipment, and I'd already sold off most of my stock to keep the poor things from starving. But when I heard about it I'd gone along to lend a hand anyhow. The days were blazin' so we had to make our hay at night. And right away I'd been cheered up, back to my old job with Muncie, bucking bales in the hot night air.

The next night after the boys were in bed the Mosleys and I were out in the yard again, stirring the fire in a pit, sitting around in lawn chairs, sharing the one cold beer I allowed myself. I told them about Ike tasting the creek water before letting Beulah have a drink. Then Clint and Eva told me about the boys tasting all the food meant for their dog. They'd fought over letting the dog sleep with them, and wouldn't feed her anything they wouldn't eat themselves. You shoulda seen them open a can and fry it in a skillet first thing in the morning. Or open a fresh bag of dry food and eat a few biscuits. When I said I'd never seen them with a dog, they looked at

43

each other, then said that their Melody had got hit by a car when she got loose last year, and was one reason they'd decided to build this new place out in the country.

I couldn't leave such a fine day on a downer, so I told them a little something I'd been holding back. Late that morning, when I was showing the boys how to pick out the horses' feet with the short blunt blade of my stock knife, I'd asked what they liked most about horses. Ike said Their ears, how they point at what they want to hear, and showed their feelings, 'cause they laid their ears back against things they didn't like. Then Mo said How they poop while they're walking, lift their tail and let go without a thought. I'd said How do you know they're not thinking, and Mo said 'Cause they never look back.

I told Clint and Eva how hanging around their boys I'd been learning things I'd forgot or never known about myself. That second morning Ike had asked me who Lady's mama was, then watched me while I tried to recall what I'd written in my little breeding book. When I started describing that fine gray mare Conchita and my old midnight black stallion Diablo, who were mommy and daddy of the gray horse they'd been riding, Ike looked up at me and said Is that written up under your lid? I snatched my hat off to show him there was nothing there. But right away he said When you're 'membering a thing, you look up and off to the left. So I thought it was under your hat somewhere. Which got us all to laughing. Lady looked up at us and snorted, a little startled. But Ike tapped his head, serious, and said It must be written somewhere only you can see.

That night I made a point of thanking this serious strong young couple for the campfire they'd lit. I said I had this thing about campfires. Maybe it was just my own cowboy upbringing, but it had been the best time for me as a boy, at the spring and fall roundups, when my Grampa and Dad would camp out with the cowboys after some long hard days in the saddle, and they all told quiet or boisterous stories around the fire, where nobody hogged the firelight. And the two bosses on the place might have sometimes known more, but usually it was cowhands that had the best tales, that told how they got to be who they were, and how they felt about it.

Clint and Eva were watching me closely, and wouldn't let it go at that, seemed like they wanted more. I said it wasn't just that shy people might open up when the light was low and flickering instead of shining down on them. Sometimes it was where hard things got said, without the noise and drama around a dinner table. You could watch who was talking out of the corner of your eye, while you poked the fire. You could say something or nothing in response, while you watched the fire eat a log whole, or saw red tongues nibble up from underneath it a little at a time. And there is something about the fire itself that's mesmerizing. Its flickering light is the oldest kind of moving picture of the night for creatures of the day huddled together for safety and comfort, till the sun comes back.

At O'Grady's Stock Barn we did come on a young gelding, a lanky red horse with white stockings, that turned up there on the third day. I set the boys up on the top rail where they could see good and not be underfoot, then checked his feet and teeth, felt his legs and listened to him breathe, and told the boys what I was looking for. I said He's a big baby, at three and a half just about like a human teenager, who already had a bunch of his grownup teeth. I put on the halter and line I'd brought and led him around a little to see if his gait had any hitches, if he was well-mannered, would follow without any ruckus. But he proved straight and sound, with a small head he held up nice, good bones and smart ways, and I was about sold on him, if the price didn't shoot up out of sight. These auctions have a way of getting away from a body, if you're all set on having your heart's desire. I asked the boys if they'd ever seen an auction, and they said no, so I said Ask your mom and dad can you go with me Saturday, if you feel like it.

So there I was with the boys early Saturday, with the gooseneck stock trailer hitched to the truck just in case. First we went to the stall and checked that the horse was still there and looked as good as he had the other day—that I hadn't missed anything. I gave the boys each a carrot to feed him, then we went to sign up at the office and get us some soda pop and a bag of salt peanuts to work on while we waited for the place to wake up. I showed the boys the little paddle I'd got, with a big number on it, that was my account for the day, but told them we had to be careful not to wave it around or we might have just bought something we didn't need, 'cause that's all the ring-men were lookin' for. I was trying not to expect anything more than just to put in a good bid when the auctioneer got around to that horse. I explained to them how sometimes there was a whole lot of interest, then the price shot up way out of sight, and sometimes it seemed like there was no interest at all, and they practically begged you to take a thing off their hands, though they hated doing that. We would just have to see.

Started out to be one of those sleepy mornings with most of the folks sitting around on their wallets, feeling a little too cushy and well-fed to bid much. I'd tried to tell the boys a little about horse-trading without scaring them off. How horse-trading can be the toughest kind of dealing. Everybody knows what you see is what you get, but not everybody knows what they're looking at. Can you read the animal's teeth, and his feet? Walk him and run him, see how he puts a foot down and picks it up? How he behaves around people, what he's avoiding or ignoring, and what he's looking right at. Some old boys have been at it so long they know some tricks there's not a soul around to teach you anymore. And why would they bother, since then you'd buy all the good ones out from under them. Besides, the old-timers would tell themselves they were offering an education that would only stand you in good stead and stick if it cost a little something by way of pain and heartache.

I didn't tell them all the other things I was looking for, like scars from a wreck that might hardly show, that still might have ruined a horse. I hadn't told Ike and Mo, but I'd also been trying to find out who that red horse belonged to, but was making no progress. The tag on him said Cloverleaf Livestock, but they weren't in the phone book, and didn't have any signs posted on O'Grady's billboard. I left the boys alone a minute and slipped back into the office to see if I could get a clue from Beverly, the cheery secretary with a long braid down her back who'd filled out my papers, since she had admired the boys, looked right at me, smiled and gave them each a candy cane. But all she knew was that the Cloverleaf outfit was not from around here, and they only brought in a few animals a year, but always paid their bills. I told her I really just wanted to find out if that little gelding already had a name, to get off on the right foot. She checked and said they hadn't given one. When I asked if he was saddle-broke, she said no, just broke to follow like most of us—which made me give her a look and a chuckle. With that I went back out and sat down with Ike and Mo, shucked some peanuts and yammered about what the auction might bring.

As we sat there working over the peanuts I told them how we did it when I was a kid. An old friend of my Grampa would buy a fifty pound burlap bag of raw peanuts. He'd soak 'em in salt water in the shell, then drain 'em and roast 'em on a cookie sheet in the oven. He told us that was how his dad had done it. His old man would put the hot peanuts back in the burlap bag and make each kid eat two peanuts shells and all, for the roughage. Then the kids could have all they wanted. And those fresh roasted peanuts still warm were the best. Even the shells didn't taste half bad.

Ike kicked his feet on the bench below ours a couple times, then said That sounds great. Why don't we do that?

I said I don't know. It might be hard to find some raw peanuts.

Mo said And a burlap bag. And wouldn't you know it right then he had us laughing.

So I said Can't hurt to have a look. If somebody has a few raw ones, we could just grow some.

Ike said Grow some?

I said Yeah, why not. They grow in the ground like potatoes, and we've got plenty of dirt. We might have to go into the city, to a health food store. Or get somebody to mail us a handful of raw ones that would still sprout. Which they hadn't thought of, but when I explained they sure liked the sound of. Mo said I thought you might could plant peanuts straight out of the can.

Then before we knew it the speakers overhead gave a loud crackle and pop and the auction was on. The boys were astounded by how fast the auctioneer talked, faster than they could figure out what he was saying, that made them giggle and whistle and spit and shake their heads. I told them there was always a little nonsense thrown in extra for no charge. They proceeded to bounce up and down, slap their cheeks and try to imitate the man in his wide cream-colored Stetson, who had a handful of papers in one hand and a mike in the other, blathering on and on. How could he make his tongue do that, Mo wondered. As he came to each item, his helpers would hold it up, or in the case of an animal, lead it around the ring down in front of the bleachers. They started with a few small items to warm up the audience—an old wooden butter churn, then a hand-crank ice cream maker, a home-made ox yoke that had been smacked with a chain to look old, then a pair of baby goats that really got the boys' attention, since Mo said they looked to be chewing tobacco. I had gotten a sheet from the office that listed everything up for sale today, and that red Cloverleaf horse was number 9.

But before the red horse got to the ring, several other horses came up first. Tall and serious, looking all around, the horses brought an air of quiet to the place. Even the ring-men slowed down, got a little quieter and stood still like they were trying to behave, though the auctioneer's patter still rattled like a hard rain over everything, just not so loud. The first horse was advertised as a top-notch cow pony, a dun-colored mare with a dark chocolate mane and tail. She was a little too good-looking for my taste, but alert and obedient to the serious woman riding her. The woman stopped, backed her up a few steps without hardly touching the reins, then cut a tight figure-eight so quick it convinced me the horse had been a serious barrel-racer a decade back when her rider was a girl. The auctioneer started her at 500 and ran the price up to 1400 without a hitch, with three serious bidders till one dropped out, then the bidding slowed. Right away the auctioneer paused, got one of the ring-men to talk up the horse a little, give some history as he called it, and sure enough he mentioned a couple barrel-racing trophies. By the time he gaveled the horse it brought 1850, and looked like a steal at that.

The boys were quiet, entranced, but I had gotten nervous. O'Grady's seemed to have gotten fancier since I was here last. I might not get near that little red horse for what I had in my pocket. The next animal was a skinny mare being ridden in blindfold by a skinny girl who looked to be 12 or 13. She rode to the middle of the ring, dropped her reins, and her horse stopped in a heartbeat. Her mare had a pink quilted jacket over her head. The girl climbed down, bowed under the mare's nose, crawled between her front legs, under her belly and out between her rear legs and tail. The horse stood stock-still. The girl ducked under her belly left to right, then back under the other way, then sprang up into the saddle and whipped her jacket off the mare's head. Then the mare stuck out one front foot, folded the other under to curtsy, and lowered her head in a bow.

The whole place erupted in applause. Ike was whistling and hooting, and both the boys were jumping up and down. The girl was blushing, but kept a straight face as she rode the mare around the ring slow as you please. Ike thought that horse must be worth a million dollars, and Mo said A million million. The mare gaveled for 850, which gave me a little hope the skinny red horse might not be out of reach. The boys were right—that little mare might not be much to look at, but she had talent, and sure was worth a second look.

A couple more serious cow horses came up, and went for serious money, then it was time for the rangy red Cloverleaf horse, led in by a hard-looking young cowhand who seemed like he knew what he was doing. Maybe he was just hard-looking because he had a big hat pulled so low no one could see his face unless they laid flat on the ground and looked up. He stopped the horse, led it around a few tight turns, backed it up with a hand to its chest, then stopped. Reading off a paper in his hand, the auctioneer described the red horse as "only started to lead and handle, but ready and willing." I could see I might have made a mistake letting the boys feed the horse those carrots, because he picked us out of the crowd right away, and watched the two boys like a hawk. And the auctioneer picked up on it too, and leveled his spiel right at us.

He tried starting the bid at 500, but got no takers. I waited till he dropped it down to a hundred for a fresh start, and raised my paddle. The auctioneer said Now we're hooked on, and right away started working the price back up. It took a little of the old stuttering doubletalk for somebody else to jump in, but then it went back and forth pretty quick. I tried to slow down my end, dug in my heels a little so it wouldn't get away from me, but the other bidder responded right away, a hundred at a time. I knew I was a little rusty and nervous when we got to four hundred before I remembered to drag my palm across my chest to signal a half to the ring-man, then the bid went to 450, then 500. How badly did the other guy want this? I kept dragging my heels, but the harder I looked the more I was convinced I was ready to buy this little horse, because he looked about like what I wanted. He hadn't been spoiled, was well-mannered, curious and polite. So I speeded up, took the bid up to 600. The other bidder was stalling now, signaled 650. Right away I raised him a hundred to 750, and that was it. The bidder in a red felt logger's hat drew a slashing finger across his throat. Going once, going twice, the auctioneer gaveled it at 750 and the little horse was mine.

The boys weren't sure what had happened till it was all done. When I grinned at them and nodded, they both started whooping, jumping up and down till I put a finger to my lips.

After the auction broke for lunch I paid at the office, got my bill of sale, and looked around for that young cowboy with the big hat but couldn't find him anywhere. I put the boys in the truck first so they wouldn't be underfoot while I led the horse around the gravel lot a little, then looped him straight into the trailer. In the basket in front I'd put a flake or two of hay, for a little welcome to chew on. Then while we were driving along smooth and slow, I asked the boys what they thought we should call him, since he'd never had a name. They sat and stared at me, then looked back and forth. Mo said it feels like too big a thing, and I said What do you mean? Mo said How do we know if we get it right? I said Horses are like people--mostly you get named in hope, then just grow into your name. Then I had a thought. What if we name him for how we feel right now? Ike said What do you mean? I said His papers had a four-leaf clover. So how about Lucky? 'Cause we got lucky to get him, and maybe he feels the same. Then we all three laughed loud and long.

Next morning was Sunday, with the new colt Lucky in a box stall in the barn, both the horse and me curious to see what was what, so I woke early, to have a look. A horse was nothing like a new piece of equipment that could just be parked and admired—he had to fit in, find his way. So I walked up, reached in the stall and gave him a carrot, and held out a couple for Lady and Beulah, out loose in the breezeway visiting with the new boy. Then I went back inside to scramble myself some eggs while I thought about having a talk with Eva and Clint, to let them know what the boys might be in for. After breakfast I decided to walk over and knock on their door, but when I looked up from my last piece of toast here they all were in a bunch on my porch in the sunshine. Ike knocked politely and said My folks wonder what the new horse looks like, and I said Why don't we go show 'em. I was feeling restless and a little lame from sitting half a day on those bleachers, and had been secretly looking forward to a stroll across the pasture to their place. But I caught up my hat and stepped out, and we walked on up to the barn.

Lady and Beulah were still hanging around outside the colt's box stall, keeping him company, as if we'd planned it that way. Ike asked me why we didn't just turn Lucky loose with the girls, and I said There's no hurry, and I'm watching close. We want him to feel safe, then he can make friends. Right now it looks like Lucky likes just having the two of them out here. Then I got a couple of currycombs and asked if the boys wanted to curry the mares, while their parents and the new colt watched. Lady and Beulah clearly liked having their hides scratched, and didn't mind being hitched up there in plain sight of the new one. Ike and Mo were doing a good job, showing off a little for their folks. When Eva asked Ike why he curried the mare, Ike said 'Cause she likes it, and it feels good. Like having your back scratched. Just then Lady snorted and nodded, and we couldn't help but chuckle.

I went to the tack room and got a couple step-ladders, so the boys could reach above the horses' shoulders. Their currying showed they'd been paying attention, and that the mares were enjoying this more than they had the first time the boys had done it. I'd told them it was a chance to look for any sores or worn patches, scabs or blisters, especially where the saddle and bridle fit. I'd told them You need to go gently at first, and see how the horse takes to it, see if there are any tender spots that might need to be looked at, maybe treated with liniment. If you see any, you be sure to show me.

At that point I invited Clint and Eva back to the house for coffee, and told the boys they could let the two mares go when they were done, but not Lucky just yet. When Ike asked if we were going to do anything more today, I said We'll just have to see. He looked at Lucky, then looked straight back at me.

Walking along to the house with Clint and Eva, I said That's gonna be the biggest thing for them to get past, the need to be patient. The boys are watching like hawks. They want it all right now, but it mostly doesn't work like that.

When we got to the kitchen, I put some water and coffee in the machine, switched it on and offered them a couple of the plain doughnuts I favored. I said I never asked if either of you have any horse history. They both shook their heads no. I said Well you've still got a leg up on your boys, since they're too small to saddle a horse for themselves. If they knew how to work together and use a step-ladder they might just get a saddle up there, but it'll take a few years till they're strong enough to cinch it tight. So for now they can't get into much trouble.

When the coffee was done and poured I asked if they had any questions. Eva said I really appreciate what you're doing with the boys. They've really taken to being around the horses. I agreed. They're both honest and curious, and mostly blurt out right what they think, so they've been no trouble. But now we're at kind of a turning point.

Clint said What do you mean?

Now that we got Lucky, we got a horse to train, that is useless otherwise. It's going to be hard on them to sit still for, but if they want to be around, all they can do mostly is watch.

Is it dangerous?

Not the way I do it. Just takes time. Depends on the horse, but mostly just lots of time.

I mentioned the skinny girl we'd seen at the auction, with her skinny horse that could do tricks. How she'd really impressed the boys. Eva said Last night we heard all about her. I told Eva I knew the girl's family, and for most of the past year that was all she did besides school work and chores.

Clint said It's not a bad thing if it keeps 'em out of trouble.

I said My thoughts exactly. Besides having skills out the other side.

Clint said Long as there's horses.

I said There's always gonna be horses. They're kinda like humans—

half tame and half wild. We need 'em around to remind us to roll in the mud once in a while and run free.

There seemed to be only one more thing to settle, but that was the hardest. Which is what was I doing here? Why me? I couldn't think how to put it, so finally just blurted out, What about the boys' grandparents? Eva looked up, started to turn toward Clint, then turned away. He said I guess we shoulda said something, but didn't know how to get into it. Ike and Mo found you for themselves, for which we're grateful, and been kind of holding our breath, hoping it might last. Then Eva chimed in. She said Clint's folks don't approve of me, never did. It's a religious thing. They wouldn't come to our wedding, said they had to work, though that was nonsense. We trade Christmas cards, and call on their birthdays, but that's about it. My father died in a car accident when I was six, and my mother works in a Winn-Dixie on the gulf side of Florida outside of Tampa, where she's trying to finish raising my brother Joey without much success. So the boys have no other family, nobody your age—not that you're all that old.

I looked them both in the face, and after a heartbeat shrugged and we laughed, that showed it was no bother, just more of the dumb people stuff. Then the boys burst in the front door and wondered what was so funny. I said Search me. I appear to have one of those faces some mamas warn you about.

After the boys had juice and a doughnut I told them I was going to work Lucky in the round pen a little, and if they wanted they could watch. But I wouldn't be riding him just yet. Ike asked Was this how you did with Lady and Beulah, and I said Mostly, though the older I get the less I'm in a hurry, and the easier it goes, but the more time it seems to take.

So first I turned Lady and Beulah out into the pasture where they'd be out of the way, then snapped a line onto Lucky's halter and walked him around to the corral. There I tied him up, went back to the barn, got an empty feed sack and closed the gate. The Mosleys all climbed up to the top rail on the other side of the ring and sat quiet. I started just leading him around the pen, using Giddyup and Whoa every time I started and stopped. I tried not to look at him directly, just let the colt follow along by using my voice and clicking my tongue. I tried not to muscle or tow him, just give him a hint then back off. Pretty soon he was following just fine, so I stopped him by where the feed sack lay on the ground, picked it up and set it on his back. It was light as a feather, but something new he didn't know, and he shivered and shook a little. I lifted it off him, and held it out so he could sniff and study it. When he was done, I held it in one hand and rubbed him with it lightly, on his back and neck, shoulders and rump. When I offered it to him again, it seemed there was nothing to fear any more. So I put it on his back, and when he settled, I clicked my tongue and we walked around the corral a couple more times, stopped and started. The feed sack lay there like he was born to it. I stopped him, rubbed him with the feed sack again, then led him to the gate, opened it, and led him back to his box stall in the barn. When we were inside the stall, I unbuckled the throatlatch on his halter and took it off, then pulled a carrot from my pocket and gave it to him. While he ate it I put a hand on his neck and just held it there.

Outside the barn I walked up to the Mosleys. Ike said Did he do good? Yep, I said. He's gonna be just fine. Has the makings of a real horse. We just got to take it nice and slow.

On Monday morning I did the same things with the feed sack, and led Lucky around the corral free and easy. I even ran him a little, changed directions and shifted gears to see could I keep him right with me, watching for clues what to do. After the feed sack, I picked up and handled his feet, to get him used to that. It must have been something the Cloverleaf people had done with him, because he wasn't startled and let me do it with no fuss. While I was working around his feet, I told the boys that it was important to get a horse used to getting his feet worked on, so his shoes could be fixed, or his hooves trimmed and filed. The last thing I did was put a bridle on him. Let him sniff it, then fed him the bit, pulled the thing up over his ears, then buckled the throat latch and led him around a couple times. The colt was calm and steady. Then I let him back to his box stall and took off his bridle.

After lunch I told the boys that afternoon we were going to show Lucky how it was done. So I led him out to the round pen so he could watch us while we saddled up Lady and Beulah, then we climbed aboard and rode off down the creek to the other end of the place. That definitely got Lucky's attention. I was sure he could probably hear us a mile away, what with the boys chirping along in high spirits back and forth. When we got back to the corral he was standing on the near side looking through the bars, nickering at the two mares, nodding and flicking his tail. It might not be much longer now.

Next morning there the boys were, bright and early. I cooked 'em each an egg and set it on a piece of toast, so they wouldn't waste away while I was finishing mine, then we walked up to the barn. Lucky seemed alert and rested, ready to get on with whatever I had in mind, so I fed him a few flakes of hay, and when he was finished I put on his bridle and walked him around the corral a while with the feed sack on his back, then got out my saddle and blanket. Showed them to him, then put the blanket on his back and walked him around another couple times, then heaved the saddle up on him. This might be a turning point. Lucky trembled a little at the weight, sensing the balance of this loose thing, but stood still, and didn't try to throw it. I walked him around, then stopped, looped the cinch under his belly and pulled it up, doubled it under the brass ring, looped it around and pulled it tight. Standing close I talked to him a little, patted and stroked his shoulder, neck and rump. Sometimes this was right where a new horse and trainer might part company. But Lucky was listening, and seemed to like what he heard and felt. There was no need to insist that he do anything.

So I took the saddle and blanket off, left them on a sawhorse I'd had Ike bring me from the barn. Then I led him into his stall, unbuckled the throat latch on his bridle, pulled it off and gave Lucky a stub of carrot I had in my pocket, and told the boys that was it for the morning. We'd just leave Lucky here in his stall, where he had food and water.

On the way to the house, Ike asked me what I'd been telling Lucky. Mo said It sounded like some kinda secret. I said I just told him what everybody likes to hear, that he was a good boy, and we were doing just fine. Both of them looked up at me, for once serious, not a ghost of a smile in-between 'em.

When the boys went home for lunch, I made myself a tuna sand-wich and ate it at the counter, then laid down on the couch. A nap has to be one of the best ways to pass the time while you calculate your next move. Whenever I get roped into a poker game I usually get dealt one hand that made me wish I could take a little nap then play my cards. Which mostly just drags out the time enough to let a body shut his eyes and see what's right there in front of him.

So it seemed like only minutes till there were two polite little knocks at the front door, though when I sat up and checked, the clock on the kitchen wall said it hadn't quite been an hour.

I let the boys in and went back to get my boots and hat, thinking about Lucky all the while. It was probably gonna be tomorrow or next week, but what about maybe today? When we got to the barn, I slipped the bridle onto Lucky, fed him the bit and buckled the throat latch, then studied if he was upset about anything. He seemed fine--head high. curious, ready for whatever might come. Relaxed enough to mostly look me right in the eye. So I spread the blanket on his back, heaved my saddle up over him, settled and cinched it down. I led him around the corral three or four times, then stopped him. Backed him up. Leaned in a little and asked him how he was doing. Patted his neck and talked to him a little more, while I watched his ears swivel round. All the signs said he was mine, long as I treated him right. So I told him what I was going to do, then I coaxed his head up, slid my left foot into the stirrup, swung up and settled. Waited a beat then clicked my tongue, and off he went around without so much as a bump in his giddyup.

The boys sitting up on the rail opposite cheered so loud they startled Lucky, made him crowhop sideways a time or two before he settled down. I held up a hand to them in warning, then rode close and told them we'd need to take it slow and easy—and quiet--to let Lucky get used to the gear and me up here and the rest. It was a lot to learn all at once, but we were getting there. We had reached the river we had to cross, and made it over the first time. Now I was going to take a short quiet ride to get him a little more used to me, and tomorrow morning we'd saddle up the mares and would all get to go see where Pipestone Creek ran. With a ride together out in the open, the horses should be about set to make their own little herd, and take us wherever we wanted.

Whole Lotta Learnin' Goin' On

Sitting around the fire pit at the Mosleys' place those long summer evenings had become a regular thing since that first time I'd talked with Clint and Eva. I watched the boys poking the fire with sticks, and saw there were still good lessons around cattle and horses, for wide-eyed boys who kept quiet. Drink upstream from the herd. Follow what their ears turn to, out ahead of their eyes. Watch what they watch, and what they sniff at, shy and ease away from. Also watch their tails, that say what they enjoy, what makes them feel restless, excited. Hear what they call out for in the night, and answer back. Watch what they feed on, that they might need more of, or what in the pasture might sicken them. Notice how their leaders stay well to the rear, look back and sniff the wind, to see what else might be on their trail.

One night after the boys had said good night, Clint and Eva wanted to talk some more about Vietnam. I'd told them about being a "lurp," how we'd go out on these Long-Range Reconnaissance Patrols for eight to twelve days, sometimes more, and hide in ambush along the trail. But Clint wanted to know how I'd got the job. So I told 'em the long and short of it.

Once out of boot camp I'd got duty papers, and was assigned to the Quartermasters' Corps. But in Orientation I soon found out that meant in-country I would be in a concrete warehouse on a big base, safe as a church mouse in a church basement. I'd noticed that the Black and Hispanic guys in my class didn't get that kind of assignment. They would be out in the hills, patrolling what they called "safe hamlets"--really just safe in daylight but getting shot at in the dark. So I went to my CO, and asked him for a real assignment. He glared at me an' said What do you mean, soldier? I said One where I do some fighting, do some good. That's really what this is about, else it's nothing. So he pulled out my file, saw I was the best shot in my weapons classes in Basic. Then he says Well okay then, it's your funeral, and signs me up for Ranger School. Of course he also calls me a nut, with an independent streak, and puts a note in my file to that effect, but that's how I got to be a "lurp."

I was serious about goin' where the action was. If I was gonna do this I oughta do it right, go where I could take the fight to them somehow and get it over with. Otherwise with soldiers all holed up behind razor wire and concrete it was gonna take forever. Of course what did I know, I was 17 when I joined up straight out of school, had to get my old man to sign for me. It was the early 70s, and the war had got to be a mess of lies and blunders so thick at that point there was no telling what was what.

I had the feeling Clint and Eva wanted to chew on what the protests and marches had been about, but it was back before their time, and I was a country boy and hadn't seen much of that anyhow. I did tell 'em about when I got off the boat in San Diego, and at the airport found an ashtray filled with the insignia some returning soldier had cut off his uniform with a razor blade-- name patch, campaign ribbons, medals, eagle buttons and all. After that we sat quiet a little.

I realized how much I'd gotten to like Ike and Mo's folks. Clint and Eva were the kind of couple that stood on their own feet, and moved under their own power. There wasn't a hint of frailty about either of them, and both knew their own minds, I could see that right off. There was always a little open space around each of them, no matter what they were doing, that their two boys could wander into or waltz through fifty times a day, step close and get a boost, a little guidance maybe, a jolt to recharge their batteries. As parents they were quiet, self-contained, with hidden abilities and energies that might never be seen unless needed and called upon. To my mind they were grownups, and good, honest parents who might have liked a little support from the likes of me and knew right what to do with it, would have welcomed a hand but really didn't much need one. They were the kind of neighbors that made me want to stand up and be counted as part of their world.

Speaking of which, since we had three horses now, that were all getting along, there was more fun to be had, as the hot part of summer came on strong. The boys tried feeding the horses everything I'd planted in the garden, till I had to ask 'em to save us a radish or two.

Then it seemed before we were half-set, summer was over and done. The boys were free and easy in the saddle, careful as I'd asked them to be. Through the summer we'd mostly gone out riding at dawn and dusk, to sidestep the heat of the day. Those climbing ropes I'd made them had worked fine. They were even taking their parents out on rides, one at a time. Clint and Eva had offered to help me with haying and harvesting oats, in return for the loan of a horse now and then, and I couldn't resist their kind offer.

Past Labor Day with the boys catching the bus at 7:10, Mo was starting first grade. When I asked what he'd learned that first day, he said that it was real school. I said How can you tell? He says No naps. Teacher says Naps and games are for babies. The second day, when Eva asked him what he'd learned, right off Mo says Rain comes out of the ground. It's 'vaporation. Comes up out of the ground, goes up in the clouds and gets heavy and falls. So the water just goes round an' round.

All of a sudden there was a whole lotta learnin' goin' on. Mo had asked Ike would he teach him what they were doing in second grade, so for the first month or so that fall that's what they did every afternoon right when they got off the bus. Ike taught his brother subtraction and cursive handwriting and some geography. Ike told me that teaching Mo really made everything stick. Said he had to have it all figured out if he was gonna 'splain it. It was always cheery asking what they'd learned, when they came over to muck out the stalls and take a little ride. Every day seemed like they had something brandnew in mind, with a wet paint sign just beggin' to be touched.

Now that it wasn't so hot, I figured to take the boys for a long ride the second Saturday, before the fall came on too strong. I tried to get Clint and Eva to come too, but they saw some good to having the time to them-selves, if I didn't mind. This would be our first real ride off the ranch, the three of us in the truck, three horses in the gooseneck trailer in back. We were going to ride on some state grazing land that sloped and curved away forever. It was just shy of two hours before we found a wide spot to pull off, where we could unload the horses, saddle up and ride. But our little herd had long gotten used to each other, and they soon settled into a nice easy stride that covered ground.

We were riding along at an easy lope when I heard something that told me how deftly the boys, for all their seriousness, could lapse into play. I don't know who started it, but as the horses cantered along, the boys' fingers were drumming on the pommel and horn of their saddles, in time with each other, in time with the horses' footfalls. Did the horses notice? I bet they did. I knew then the boys could be twenty or thirty or fifty, and still be mes-merized by the rhythm and music of the ride. That's just how some cowboys were, their days mostly unrushed, not overburdened enough to lose track of the pleasure to be had just riding along, on the way somewhere not much more vital in the scheme of things than right where you were at the time.

After an hour or two I stopped, stepped down, and Ike and Mo climbed down too. We passed around the canteen, took a drink and had a look. I gave them each a granola bar, then said Where do you think we are? Ike said The middle of nowhere. I said And what if I take one more step? He looked up at me, solemn, sure I must be funnin'. Then Mo grinned. I said What? And he said There's no middle to nowhere. Everything is so far away it all looks the same. There's no places out here, not a thing people ever made or did. Not a doorstep nor tin can, hardly a flat stone. We can't even see the road we came in on. The nowhere of it all goes on and on.

The boys had never been out like this where they could practically follow the curve of the earth, where on a clear day they could practically see forever. Not a horse nor a human in sight, no fences or roads, no beer bot-tles or garbage, just a sprinkling of cattle way off near the horizon, that Mo said looked like ants. Ike said How far you figger we can see? I said Twenty or thirty miles. Unless there's a mountain or something. I pointed at those dark little specks. You could ride hard till dark and not get there.

That day we rode on another few miles, mostly follow-the-leader, with Ike aboard Beulah the oldest in the lead, then Mo on Lady, then me on young Lucky bringing up the rear. But then for some stretches we spread out side by side, and rode that way awhile since the boys were starting to get better telling what the horses liked. When we stopped for another stretch I asked why the horses did it that way. Ike said they liked to play follow the leader, step right where the leader stepped, but then they also liked seeing each other, liked to fall in step side by side, every beat nodding their heads. It was like a play race, or maybe a parade. Here the ground was pretty flat, the prairie eaten and beaten down, so there wasn't much to step in or trip over. As we rode along fanned out that way, up jumped a coyote right in front of us, snatching at a mourning dove that was swooping low over the ground. We were so close we could hear its jaws clack as it missed. The horses didn't seem bothered at all, just side-stepped a second or two, then carried on. I asked the boys if they saw what she was chasing, but they were too surprised to notice much. Mo said What makes you think it's a she, and I said The time of day. It's when her pups likely nap.

The sun was getting pretty low when we finally slowed to a stop, then turned around. I'd planned it like this, and wanted to see how the boys would take to a little night-riding. I got some apples, sandwiches and snacks out of my saddle bags, took off the bridles, buckled on halters with a lead on each, and let the boys feed the horses an apple and a carrot apiece, then get a bite for themselves. I told them I hoped they weren't too hungry, because I'd asked their folks if they wouldn't mind eating a little late. Ike says What for? I says So you get to see the magic show.

I checked the saddle cinches, put the bridles back on, and we mounted up to head back. Beulah willingly took the lead again, and we let her set the pace. The boys sank into the quiet, and I kept quiet myself, just let 'em find the way as the twilight came on, where the purple and lavender rose into the sky and faded in the distance out ahead. Then there was just the old creak and jingle of saddles and bridles, and the drumbeat of hooves as the horses followed along, and settled into the ride. Then off to our left all at once we could hear the yip of coyotes from a den. Mo said You think they're calling their mama? I said Sure, but they sound pretty grownup, like they're about ready to go hunting for themselves.

As the sunset faded to nothing, I asked the boys were they watching the trail. Ike said I don't know, I can't hardly see a thing anymore. Then I said, I think your Beulah is doing the driving for us all. And I think she likes it, 'cause she's doing such a good job. If you feel around for your hands, you can tell we're all taking it easy, not steering anything, giving the horses their heads. Letting them take us where they want to, where they think best. And with no landmarks at all, they're mostly just remembering and smelling out the way we came. If it was snowing, or a dust storm, or pitch dark like this, that is all we can do, and be glad of it, because in low light and no light, they can see better than we can.

As we rode along it got dark enough we started to spot a few bright stars. I showed the boys the Big Dipper and how to use its two front stars to find the North Star, and talked about how to use it to tell time and find our way. Right now we were almost heading due north, though I didn't bother pulling out my pocket compass. Then in a little while the moon rose, low and creamy up ahead. It wasn't quite full, but full enough to be welcome. All at once the boys seemed to wake up. They got chatty, talking about the coyotes and nighthawks and owls calling back and forth all over this ghostly prairie. It wasn't long before we could see the truck and trailer parked off the pale, empty road, still and solemn like they'd been carved out of soap, with no life of their own. We rode up and stepped down, unsaddled and loaded the horses in the trailer. Then we got in the truck and sat quiet in the dark a minute with the windows down, just looking and listening, hearing and feeling the horses behind us shift around, getting settled, feeling the trailer sway a little in the night wind. When they were calm I fired up the truck and eased back around to head home.

The long truck ride stayed pretty quiet until Mo said Mr. Brick, what was it you wanted to show us? I said Just exactly what you saw--but mostly heard, and felt. That only real cowboys get acquainted with. Then I asked Do you think the horses liked it? Or were they scared? The same instant both said Not a bit! And why do you think that is? Ike said 'Cause they like being out here together. And they like this kind of country. I said Open range? Ike nodded, said Yep. I said This is the kind of land they prob'ly dream about, without fences, with all kinds of other animals out there pokin' around in the dark. With the wind sighing and tearing through the grass, with a little pink heat lightning way off in the hills, with yipping coyotes and nighthawks and owls who-hooing and the like.

Then out of the dark Ike says What if Beulah couldn't see so good out here? I say Then one of the other horses woulda taken over. You remember those times when the horses slowed down, then stopped a second, looked around at each other? We couldn't see it, but that's what they were doing. That was them all checking on each other. Askin' Beulah if she was doin' all right. Then Beulah went on. Mo says They sure found the trailer and truck. I say You got that right. You know what that is, don't you? I let the question hang a long time. Some call it herd mind. How they learn to trust each other, and think as one. Sometimes they even include us.

When we pulled into the ranch, I gave the horn a tap to greet Clint and Eva, who were out by their fire pit. In short order we backed out the horses, tossed off their gear, curried and wiped them down, then put them in their stalls and fed and watered them. The horses were tired and happy, and quiet as the boys were as we walked over to the Mosley place. But then in a breathless rush their folks got to hear all they saw and heard and did. They didn't even sit down to eat their chili dogs, just danced around the fire and pointed up at the moon, talked about how big and round the world had to be, with its Big Dipper and a million billion stars. They even started doing cartwheels round the yard, took turns playing Big Dipper, that Mr. Brick said is really a big ol' bear. And all the while Eva and Clint hardly offered to answer a word. They were both smiling so hard in the firelight I knew we'd have to take them along, soon as I found us a couple more good horses.

Somewhere along in there when the boys got to tellin' for the third time about that coyote leapin' and snappin' after that mourning dove I dozed off, and next thing Clint was nudging me to offer a nightcap, which I had to decline. Eva had taken the boys in to bed, but said she'd be right back, said she wanted to hear how I could make magic out of pritnear anything. When she got back she said she'd had to ask the boys if they'd been scared out there. Ike said Not for a minute. When she said Why not, Mo said 'Cause the horses were drivin'. And there was the bunch of us all thinkin' the same.

When I got up to toddle home to bed, behind me Clint said One more thing--did you ever pull out your flashlight? I turned around, saw the firelight glint in their eyes, and said Nope. Nor the compass. Never touched 'em, never mentioned 'em. Why mess with a good thing?

The So-Called Facts of Life

With school coming up early Monday, for Sunday dinner we grilled some hamburgers and baked some beans and made an early night of it. When the boys came out in their pajamas to bid us good night, Ike said he had a question. I said Sure, what's that? And he said Is a horse a wild animal or a tame animal? I said That's a good one, that could take us all night. Let me ask you this: Is a dandelion wild or tame?

I couldn't say for sure.

Well, if it can plant itself and grow itself, and in the end make more of the same without any help but the sun and rain and what it pulls up outa the ground, I'd say it's wild.

But how about horses?

They're big strong animals that run faster than us. So how about just the short answer? Horses were all wild until about six thousand years ago, when the first ones got caught and tamed, in the steppes of Eastern Europe and Asia, which is open rolling grass prairie like ours, and over the years they got so they didn't mind being around people. They're still shy and like to be in herds, where they can be warned of danger and run away. But when the Spanish explorers first arrived in the Americas, a bunch of their horses got loose, and roamed in herds on their own for over a hundred years, till the southern tribes, Commanche, Cheyenne and Ute, started catching and riding them.

Mo said How'd they do that? I said How do you think? Mo said They prob'ly used a rope. I said Not bad, but then Ike had an idea. He said Maybe they stole some babies and raised 'em up by hand, and treated 'em right. I said Raised 'em up by hand--that's an awful good guess, that I think is just about right. It's like tame animals made a deal with us a long while back, and have a job that lets them live around us and help us, and get helped in return, like dogs and cats. Eva said How about let's dream about it for now, and talk more tomorrow. With that the boys said goodnight and Eva went to tuck 'em in.

After the boys were in bed we got to talking about what the boys might be like in a few years. I told the Mosleys I was hopeful, since I'd had a cowboy English teacher when I was in sixth grade, a couple years before I could finally get my knee high enough to boost a saddle up on the back of a horse. There were only a few of us in the class who grew up on farms an' ranches, that knew what he was talking about, but to the other kids it was like he'd stamped our passports to the grown-up world. Around town Mr. Bud Avery looked like he might be a bookkeeper or librarian--a balding man with horn-rimmed glasses, in his fifties, kinda pear- shaped, who walked a little bow-legged, but still had a twinkle in his eye and some good stories if you caught him right. That year we lived for Friday afternoons when we'd finished the week's work early, so he'd settle in his rocking chair for the final hour, and spin out what we called his cowboy adventures. Some Fridays he even wore the gear--boots and black Frisco jeans with a tooled belt and snap-button western shirt, with a vest and black hat and string tie. He'd tell stories about roundups when he was a boy, how he spent his first whole night in the saddle riding round hundreds of cattle, pinching and slapping himself, bitin' his tongue so as not to doze and fall off in the cactus. He said That's before I realized I could sing songs to stay awake. He told about the tricks cowhands would pull on each other, especially pranks played on a sound sleeper around a campfire, like squirting canned shaving cream on his fingers, then tickling his nose with a straw. He'd answer questions even we ranch kids wouldn't hear talked of at home. One Friday he told about him and two other cowhands roping a bull to load him in a trailer where he didn't want to go. He said they each got a rope on him, then used what he called a twitch, a metal grabber with a wingnut in the handle you tightened, that clamped that bull by the nose, to lead him where they wanted. But once they took hold of him they couldn't let go till the job was done, or he'd a stomped 'em to jelly. Even with that thing in his nose he was so mad he was too strong for them. It took all they had plus another three or four hands to get him in and shut the gate on him. Then somebody still had to reach through the bars and get that damn twitch off. He said they never used it again.

One time in class I asked him What was the best way to catch a horse, and he said Get one that comes when you call. The kids all laughed but I was serious. I said how do you do that? He said If you can, you start the day they're born. If you treat 'em right, handle 'em like you was their mama, and never make their real mama mad, pretty soon they'll practically follow you around. 'Course, it helps if you got all the time in the world, and a treat in your pocket. But then, after school with no one else around he waved me over and gave me the kind of straight answer I'd need. He said Never chase a horse afoot, unless it's got a rein or a line trailing off it. Said he'd take off his belt and hold it behind his back while he pretended to have a treat for the horse in his other hand. He said Make it real in your mind. Give it some shape, play with it, pretend to take a little bite. Smack your lips. When the horse let him close enough, he'd loop his belt around the horse's neck, buckle it, pull up his feet and hang his whole weight on the belt till the horse let himself be led where he needed to go. But then he said As soon as I can, I give him a real treat to put his mind at ease.

Unlike some of the kids, I had smart people on the home place to ask, my dad and granddad, but they didn't take me seriously. So it felt like every question at home turned into a joke on me. The cowboy still in Bud Avery would answer anything, if it was a real question, and I could catch him right, had done my work, and wasn't just burnin' daylight. He'd even talk about the birds and bees, breeding horses and cattle, whatall that was about, and how it worked. I realized my family had been keeping us kids away from that kinda stuff, like we might go gettin' ideas from watching a stallion mount a mare in heat, that never looked much like fun, to us anyhow. I know now the real truth was it was plain dangerous, like Mr. Avery loading that bull in a trailer. Most of the older hands I've known have been kicked or stepped on around a bull or stallion. And Mr. Avery had a finely honed sense of how far he might go in the telling. He'd end talk about breeding livestock by saying 'Course I'm not gonna draw you a picture. That should be plenty if you keep your eyes an' ears open. And don't you go askin' your mom.

At which point I stopped, turned to Eva and Clint, and said Maybe we oughta talk about that. What do you think about me talkin' over that kinda stuff with the boys? They looked at each other a minute, then Eva said I think it's fine coming from you. They know you know what's what, and are tryin' to keep 'em safe. And you've got a pretty good record so far.

But when it comes to the birds and the bees and all that, wouldn't you rather I tell 'em to ask you? At this point Clint spoke up suddenly, said Hellfire, I'd rather hear what you had to say anyhow. We laughed, but then I said I really don't want to be doin' your job. So you gotta give me somethin' to work with. How about if you tell me how you got to hear about the birds and the bees for yourselves?

So Eva said when she was 12 she came home from school and told her mother a boy had kissed her on the school bus. She hadn't even liked the boy, hadn't felt a thing, but it turned ugly when all the other kids started chanting and egging him on. The bus driver slammed on the brakes, hit the flashers, and made everybody sit in their assigned seat before he'd go another inch. At which point my mother got all upset. She started shouting and pointing her finger at me, saying Young lady, we are taking no chances with you from here on out! Then she called the school nurse, Mrs. Cutler, and made her take me out of class next day and explain what my mom called "The Facts of Life." She was a big lady in a white uniform with huge bosoms and too much makeup and perfume, who had a big text book open on her desk with color pictures of people's insides, and a list of fancy medical words she'd written down on a clipboard. But Mrs. Cutler was no fool. I went in, took one look at the book and started crying. And I didn't stop till Mrs. Cutler shut the book, and said There, there now, missy, I guess you're not ready for this. So it'll just have to be our little secret, won't it, dear. Then she gave me a handful of tissues, told me to blow my nose, and go on back to class.

Clint said So you never did get the talk? Eva gave a little smile and shook her head. So how did you find out about it all? She said How do you think? The way everybody does, first from friends, a little at a time. Then groping around in the dark back seat of some boy's car. He said That ain't hardly fair. She said Okay for you, Mister Mosley. Let's hear your story.

Clint said Well, you know mine can't be much. My parents sent me to a religious grade school, which was pretty strict, with no real science to speak of, not much history, and never a word about sex. It got so the seventh grade kids would ask questions in religion class to try and trip up the teacher, who was studying to be a minister, but already wore the white starch collar. So one day this smart girl Tammy asked Mr. Cox a question about Lot and his daughters. She said Isn't having sex with your daughters a no-no, even if they did get their father drunk? Mr. Cox said Where are you getting your facts? She said Out of the Bible, Genesis Chapter 19: verse 30 to 38. He got out his Bible, thumbed around a little, then said I'll have to get back to you on that. And with that the kids all laughed and carried on nonstop until the bell rang. Next day Mr. Cox was gone. And the day after that there was an old minister, Reverend Arburthnot, up front, and the class became a study hall for the rest of the year.

I asked Clint if his parents ever said a word about the Facts of Life. He said They thought their job as parents began and ended with church on Sunday and food on the table. They thought children should be seen and not heard. They never had much interest in grades, or health, or what we studied, they just wanted to be sure nobody flunked and had to repeat a grade, which would be a cause for shame. There was one thing, though. My dad liked baseball, and got into it with my coach a time or two, because he thought I showed promise, and the coach's kid got to play first base every game, while I was stuck in the outfield.

This wasn't turning out like I'd thought. And right then Eva said it was my turn. So I said You already know my rancher dad and rancher grandfather were a pair of hard cases. They let me believe that TV wrestling was real from the first, with an honest good guy in a white hat and a bad guy in a black hat that cheated when the ref wasn't lookin'. So I never got a real talk about the facts of life that wasn't an excuse for a joke. About all they ever did was make me recite how you tell a mare in heat. "She tosses her tail up, and winks her vulva, pisses a lot and gives the stallion the eye." They made me learn that word for word--which is useful, but not the whole story by a long shot. Whenever one of 'em would ask me how you tell a mare in heat, I'd rattle it off and the two of 'em would bust out laughing till I got up and left.

My only real instruction came at 17 thanks to the U.S. Army and Sergeant Hardesty. When we got done with basic training, and were about to get our first weekend pass, we were standing there at Parade Rest while Hardesty the top sergeant had somebody pass out these little kits. Each one had four condoms in it, and a little booklet. And he stood there and said The booklet was our friend, then said Put the rubbers in your wallet or uniform pocket, where you can get at 'em quick. He even said Do it now, and waited a minute while we did. Then he said You men are trained killers, and your job is to be an effective fighting force. But if you catch a venereal disease somewhere off post, if you get the itch and a discharge, and start to burnin' down there, you can look up what it means for yourself, and get treated sooner than later. It's all in that little book. But believe you me, you'll be distracted to say the least. You won't be an effective fighting force, you'll be anything but a trained killer, you'll be practically worthless. So use protection, have it with you at all times, and don't get yourself and the folks you care about all loused up. A baby is a wonderful thing, a delight and a blessing, but it's nice to be able to choose when and where to have one, and this way you get to choose. I got only one more thing to say--your job in-cludes safety first, so stay safe and play nice. See you at 0600 Monday, right on the spot where you're standin'. Dis-missed!

Clint and Eva laughed so hard they about fell on the ground. When they caught their breath they were still so riled up they had to hear more of my time in the Army. So I told them how I spent that weekend pass. I'd hitched a ride into town to find something to drink. But it seems I went out the wrong gate at Fort Benning and picked the wrong town. I'd never been much of a drinker, only a bottle of beer at a party now and then, but this little town was over the Alabama line in a dry county, with no taverns, and no beer for sale anywhere. They let me out on the courthouse steps in the hot sun in my uniform, and I went up to a little old feller in overalls and a straw hat settin' on a bench in the shade, introduced myself and asked if he knew where I might find me a drink. He said Will moonshine do? and I said Sure, though I had no idea. He said four bucks a pint, and I said Fine with me. He said You got the money? and I reached in my pocket and showed him. So he turned around slow and careful like he was scoutin' for spies, then pointed over to an alley off the square, and said he'd meet me there in twenty minutes. I sat down and waited a little, then walked up the alley, and there he was, under a tree. He stuck out his hand, and I gave him my four dollars, and he pulled a pint mason jar from his pocket. Then he unscrewed the lid and handed me the jar, and made a little wiggle with his fingers toward his mouth, like he was playing an invisible tuba. I reached for the lid, but he wouldn't give it to me. He said You gotta drink it here and now. I said I might want to drink it later, but he said he needed his jar back, besides which it was evidence. He said That's how we do things hereabouts, to confound the law. He says Drink all you want, but it's gotta be now, and I'll be takin' my jar.

Well, I'd never had any moonshine, never laid eyes on the stuff. The boys in the barracks made jokes about Kickapoo Joy Juice which was Li'l Abner's name for illegal corn whiskey, but this looked to be clear as rain water. So I tipped back my head and poured some down. And in that hot sun my head swirled. Something in me softened and flashed and started to move in slow motion like my brain had just grown a thousand tiny legs. My knees turned to rubber. The man in overalls and straw hat kept making that little swirling motion with his fingers toward his mouth.

He said, Down the hatch, buddy. I ain't got all day.

But I was already drunk as a snake, drunk as a possum chasin' a bobcat in the weeds. I lifted the jar and tried to hit my mouth, but poured a bunch down my shirt front. It had no taste, no color, was warm as blood, but sure had a kick. I was stunted and blasted. I put my left hand up to shade my eyes, and hooked a thumb over my left ear so I wouldn't lose it. The man stared up at me, said Does the trick, don't she. I tried to offer him a dollar for his jar and lid, but nothing came out of my mouth but half my tongue. He made the finger motion, trying to hurry me along. I poured a little into the hole in my face, tried rinsing my teeth with it, thinking maybe that way it wouldn't be so hot. But nothing worked. A howl came up outa me, like a dog who'd got his tail stomped. My throat felt like a furnace. I pulled my lips back and blew air out through my teeth. My neck and knees had the shivers. I slid to the ground with the jar still upright. I congratulated myself I hadn't spilled a drop except what I'd sloshed on my belt buckle rinsed off the finish. I tried to lean against the tree, but hunched around and couldn't find it. The man bent down and took the jar from my hand. It still had enough of the clear stuff to poison two men and a boy. He tipped his head back and let his adam's apple work around the last of it. Then he gave a little head shake like a wet dog and said Sorry, just bidness, an' the law needs confoundin', else it might ketch us. While he shook out the jar and screwed on the lid I asked if I could pay him to ride me back to the fort. He said What for? I said To lay me down somewhere I won't get run over, 'cause I been snakebit fixin' to die, and need to go where someone'll find me, that knows where to ship the remains. So for a sawbuck he did.

Horse-Breaking Rivers

One of those nippy January nights the Mosley boys were camping in their yard, breakin' in their new tent and sleeping bags from Christmas, and we were having a pretty noisy time of it around the fire. Eva and Clint were there too, having a cup of tea. As usual we got to talking, and I recalled another thing my old cowboy teacher Bud Avery had told me in the sixth grade, that I'd never found a use for. That's just how it is sometimes, you get a lesson you keep tucked away, that won't make sense for years, if ever, because it's so particular, in a world so wide and various. I had asked him once after school how he broke horses to ride, and he said on the home place where he grew up in the middle of New Mexico, in the hills outside what used to be San Marcial till it washed away, they'd had an arroyo full of lava rocks from the size of a baseball to the size of a grapefruit or soccer ball, mostly round and hard, that was hell on the poor horses' feet. No telling how those rocks got there. It was like a dry river bed that maybe used to run hard enough to tumble stone into cannonballs. More likely they came out of the ground hot and just rolled along while they cooled. Or maybe fell hot into water that ran down through that draw once upon a time. However it happened, the spot was no bargain for a cowhand in boots to walk on either. Still, the hands had a good use for that little valley that was worthless otherwise, that we steered around and shied away from, cow and horse and man.

He said it didn't look it, but turned out to be the perfect spot for breakin' horses. The first time there, a horse could hardly stand up or stand still for all the rocks turning underfoot. So we'd saddle and bridle a green horse, and lead it the mile or so from the barn to that rocky draw. And as we'd approach we'd have to speed up a little so the horse didn't just stop at the edge, 'cause we needed to get her out a ways, good and stranded. All these young horses would behave the same, spread their legs out like a hog on ice, tryin' to hold still, with their knees shakin' somethin' awful. Then we'd ease up into the saddle like we're climbin' a rickety step-ladder set to collapse out from under us. And the horse might go into a crouch, try a hop or two, or not. But we'd just sit and wait 'em out, keep her head up, and pretty soon the poor young horse would accept the burden on her back and pick her way, and we'd let her, and help her along best we could. And by the time we got out onto flat ground again, the horse was mostly done buckin', set to follow our lead.

Once in a while a young horse might lose her head, and make a wild jump or two, lose her footing, and go down. Then came the tricky part. If you stayed in the saddle then you might land wrong yourself, so you needed to watch, keep the reins up and be set to jump free. You'd need to jump toward the horse's head, maybe over her back, and away from her hooves that could finish you. Then as she got up you'd climb right back on, and keep her head high so she didn't try jumping again. It usually took an hour or so of floundering around in what the boys called that Rocky River, till she'd be gentled to ride from then on. She just had to surrender, decide to trust you to get her through, no matter the predicament. She might only have to do this once, let you climb up without trying to throw you, and that surrender and acceptance worked like old-time religion, where all at once you saw the light and were saved

I'd asked Bud Avery Wasn't it dangerous, couldn't a horse break a leg? He chuckled and said What's not dangerous around horses, and a cowboy could break a leg too. But the animal's smart enough to know it's in a real fix, the worst kind of footing, so always took it slow, and it was safer than it looked. He said he never knew of a horse to be lost on that dry gulch.

But he told us everybody limped around with sore hips and knees and ankles for a few days after a ride on that damn rocky riverbed, man and horse. But to them it was nothing compared to being tossed off a green horse in the corral, that felt like falling off a barn roof, where the cowhand took the full beating and the horse weren't hardly bothered to speak of. Mr.

Avery said it was a trick he'd learned as a boy from an old Comanche cowboy on the place, that everyone called Perdido. Perdido would give a little laugh when anybody said his name, although no one else ever dared make a sound. I assumed it was because his name meant "lost soul" or "hopeless one," some kind of religious warning or curse. El Perdido rode off to hell with El Diablo. Anyhow, Perdido had told the cowboys how in his grandfather's day this place used to be known by The People all round this country, who called it Horse-Breaking River. He said they had to make use of whatever they had in dry country, when they couldn't find water enough to break horses. Which turned out to be two ancient secrets in one. If they had a river or tank or lake deep enough, the rider would blindfold the horse and lead it into water till it had to swim. When it was on tiptoe, just on the edge of floating, the rider would climb on its back and snatch off the blindfold, then let the horse exhaust itself without hurting the rider. It usually didn't take long for the horse to accept its situation and let the man ride it from then on.

Perdido said in the old days horses seemed more content to remain around the People, and seldom strayed. The People were fierce warriors then, and near camp the horses felt safe from mountain lions, wolves and bears. The People always lived near good water and grass, and took care to move on before either got scarce. Their great Comanche Trail ran north from the Rio Grande through the water holes and rivers of west Texas up to their hunting grounds in Oklahoma, Colorado and Kansas. The young ones who kept watch over the herd, set to warn of predators and thieves in the night, were called Horse-Watchers and Horse-Catchers, until they were sent into the desert alone to have a vision and find their real names. Then they could ride with grownups on the hunting and raiding parties.

Well, at that I stopped and looked around to see if it was time for bed. But all of a sudden the boys were wide awake. Ike said why don't we ever do that? I said We don't have any deep water, or a wash fulla cannonballs an' such, and besides, I think there's a better way, without scaring the horse quite so bad. We ease along and let the animal see what we're doing, and let it make the choice to join us or not.

Ike sat quiet a minute, then said Mr. Brick, did you ever have a horse you couldn't ride?

I have to say as a matter of fact I once did, but it was an odd situation. When I was 12 one Saturday I was hangin' out in the cookhouse watchin' the cooky Bartolo bakin' some pies. He'd mixed several kinds of frozen berries together, sweetened 'em with honey, cinnamon, nutmeg, raisins an' such, rolled out some pie crust and put six pies in the oven-- and they were smellin' like heaven. The boys were out in our biggest field doctorin' some heifers, maybe ten miles away, and he was fixin' them some noonday dinner. But then all of a sudden he dropped a pan and sat down on the floor. Said he wasn't feelin' so good, said he was dizzy, and had to lie down. There was nobody else around but me, so I got him a glass of water, 'cause he was lookin' hot an' sweaty, and fetched him a pillow off the couch. Then I told him I was going to get help. I ran up to the big house and told Elena the housekeeper, and she went in to tell Grampa and Dad. They called the aid car to come take him to the hospital that was eighty miles away. I ran back to Bartolo and said help was coming, and meanwhile could I get him anything. He said Could you pull those pies outa the oven, an' watch out you don't burn yourself. I could smell them good now so got some pot holders an' pulled 'em out lickety-split, and didn't drop a one. Bartolo said Good boy, you already know not to dawdle when it's a matter of pies. Then he leaned back and shut his eyes. But then all at once he opened his eyes and tried to sit up.

Almost forgot, this here lunch has got to get out to the boys. Think you could do that?

What do you need me to do?

Well, the boss Donny harnessed Big Bertha and hitched her up to that little wicker governess cart for me, since I don't sit a horse so good no more, never mind packin' lunch. She should be tied up out in front of the barn. You just grab that box of sandwiches and snacks there and put the pies in another box and set 'em all in the cart, then latch the little door and drive out the road to where they're workin'. You can't miss it. Be sure and put a handful a forks and plates and a spatula into the box with the pies.

I ran around the kitchen gathering what he told me, then made a couple trips out to the two-wheeled cart that I can't remember to have ever seen before. It seemed to be woven and stitched out of some kind of sticks, then painted bright apple green. Between the shafts was the biggest horse I'd ever seen, that I'd never seen before either. A huge gray mare, that musta been over eighteen hands high, and wide as she was tall, standin' there still as a statue, eyein' me. Tied to the hitchin' rail by the barn, set to go.

I went back inside and Bartolo was still lying there on the floor with his eyes closed. When he sensed me flutterin' around, he opened his eyes and said What?

I never drove me a horse before.

There's nothing to it. You can ride a horse, can't you?

I nodded.

Bartolo said Just remember giddyup and whoa. Click your tongue to get her going. Hold onto the reins between your thumbs and forefingers like this--he showed me with his apron strings--and keep just a little feel on the bit, but not too much. You don't wanta hurt her mouth. She's a good horse, just take it nice an' easy. An' remember to get you some lunch for your trouble, and a piece a pie for yourself.

And with that I was off. I untied Big Bertha, fed the reins back to the cart, then led the horse out to the road, climbed in and clicked my tongue. But when she didn't budge I called out her name, slapped the reins on her back like I'd seen the boys do, and off we went.

Bertha was a lotta horse, and lumbered into a canter without me hardly askin' her. But the springs on the wicker trap were pretty soft, and I had to sit sideways while driving, so I was sliding all over. I'd never rode in anything like this little cart before, and rockin' side to side and front to back was like I was out to sea in a little square boat. The road was gravel and narrow, with no ditches on either side. That horse was so tall and wide I had to lean out to look around her, but there was no one in the road up ahead to run into anyhow. The whole cart was tipped back and woulda worked better if they'd put a pony in the shafts instead of Big Bertha. But there was a little hinged door at the back that I had latched good, so the lunch wouldn't fall out in the road.

I knew the way well enough, since I'd ridden that road several times before. About halfway there was a big gate I had to stop and get down to open, then led Bertha through and shut after us. The big mare was well-mannered, but I was takin' no chances and kept one long rein in my hand as I swung the gate shut behind us. But there was somethin' about the squeak of that rusty ol' gate she didn't much care for, and she turned her head and rolled her eyes like there was trouble back there somewhere, that I thought might include me.

I climbed back in an' latched the little door, then shook the reins an' Bertha took off, but this time she started really runnin' like there was demons on her tail, and I was gettin' thrown all over, and it took me a mile to slow her down to where I wasn't holdin' on for dear life. A couple miles more and the field hove in sight where the cowboys were workin'. They had all the heifers in a corral. I waved and brought Bertha to a stop near a waterin' trough that was fed by a windmill. I let her have a good long drink, then tied her and carried the two boxes over to where the boys had their tools an' medicines laid out on a folding table.

When I opened the boxes the sandwiches were all fine, because they were in waxed paper bags to begin with, but the pies had slid all over, and I had to kind of shovel the filling and crust back into the pie pans. Donny the foreman gave me a hand with the spatula, and hacked up the pies into quarters, put each on a plate and handed them around. They were messy but still warm, and no one seemed to mind. In fact, everyone including me ate their pie before we even studied our sandwiches, which turned out to be meatloaf with ketchup and mayonnaise. Donny asked me where Bartolo was, and I said he was sick, and had had to lay down on the floor till the medics got there. I felt bad I couldn't tell the boys what seemed to be wrong with him.

The boys enjoyed their lunch anyhow, and loaded all the dirty plates and forks in the boxes, that I put back in the little wicker cart. Then I untied Bertha and turned her around to head home. I waved to the boys, climbed up and latched the little back door, then started off. But after a mile or two the road climbed a hill and made a turn to the right, and just as we got to the top and went into the turn, the left wheel came off, and the cart dropped down on the axle and dumped me. I still had the reins in my hands, and started shouting Whoa, whoa while Bertha dragged me along a little ways. But she stopped when I got loud enough, and looked around at me as I scrambled to my feet. I looked at the cart and saw there must have been a cotter pin fell out, or maybe never was one to begin with but shoulda been, and the nut had worked its way off. I tied Bertha to a small tree and looked around for the nut and cotter pin but couldn't find either one, so decided I'd have to take Bertha out of the shafts and ride her home. It took me a little while to figure how to get her loose from the cart, take those two little hooks off the back end of her harness tugs that went to the singletree, then I walked her forward out of the shafts while I lifted the left side to give her room to move. She was mannerly all this while, but then shook herself all over, once she was free, as if to say she'd like to be shut of the harness while we're at it.

I studied the situation, and figured I was at least eight miles from the barn and there was no good way to climb up on Bertha's back. I tried hoisting myself up on the tugs, using the reins and her collar to pull myself up, but Bertha didn't want me there. She shook me off, but then didn't run away, just stood over me as I sat up, then got to my feet again. I tried her from the other side, but she wouldn't let me up that way either. I began to think maybe she'd never been ridden--as the cowboys would say she wasn't saddle-broke. And harness-broke didn't count, far as she was concerned.

So I gave it one more try, and Bertha shook me off again, this time swirling her head like she had a fly in her ear. When I looked up there she stood like she wondered what was keepin' me. So I picked myself up again, looped up the long reins over my shoulder, clicked my tongue, and started on down the road leading her home. As I plodded along I remembered the gate into the big pasture that was maybe three miles off by now. I might could climb up the gate and get on her back--if she'd let me. It was a plan that at least kept us moving.

Of course I was hopin' someone else might happen along who could make Bertha see eye to eye, but no one did. When I got to the fence and the gate I opened it, led Bertha through, then pulled her back toward me while I closed the gate, which made that screeching sound again, and Bertha rolled her eyes, but this time seemed like she might just be bored. Then I scrambled up the gate and tossed a leg over her, and grabbed for those two brass balls on the ends of the hames on her collar. It was a good thing I did because I hadn't reckoned on her back being wide and flat as a card table. She gave her shoulders a shrug and her hind end a bump and I tumbled off in a heap. I still had the reins looped in one hand, and this giant horse standing over me, studyin' as if to say No hard feelings, but no free rides: that's the rules.

I was surprised she hadn't run off. She was so smart it seemed like she was curious to see what I might try next. But I was fresh out of ideas. I didn't yet have sense enough to be scared, so I studied her from down there, congratulated that giant horse on her patience, got up again slower than ever and checked if anything might be broke, then clicked my tongue, and she followed right along for the next couple hours, all the way back to the barn. By then it had begun to seem like she had every right to reject my claim as her boss, since I had been promoted up out of nowhere. I studied the situation one more time, had no hard feelings, patted her shoulder and tied her to the hitching post where I'd found her, since I couldn't have got her bridle off without a step ladder anyhow. I went into the cook house, where as I expected Bartolo was long gone. So I hobbled up to the big house a little slow since my joints were startin' to stiffen up from being dumped on the ground more times than I could count. There I learned from Elena the housekeeper that Bartolo'd been taken off in a little red truck with lights and sirens, and wouldn't be back for a couple days, so I should tell the hands they were on their own, as far as grub was concerned. Somehow while she was telling me all this I sat down in a chair, leaned back against the wall and fell asleep, and never heard what was wrong with the poor cook till next morning.

Ike and Mo really liked that story, but wanted to know what was the matter with Bartolo. I said a bum ticker. But after a couple of days of eatin' their own cooking, when the cook came through the door the boys hailed him like visiting royalty, though after that we all spent a couple weeks tiptoeing around him like he might explode, before things got back to normal. I never did ride that big gray horse, found out they'd bought her for some huge gray old man to ride, but he'd never showed up for his cowboy vacation. He was the CEO of a breakfast food company who liked his own products too much. Which was maybe just as well, since nobody else ever rode her either, though most of the boys said they tried. Bartolo finally told me Bertha's secret--she was just too big around to get aholt of, and not a one of the boys could hang on for even a rodeo minute. So they made up the excuse she was too old to learn, which was pure nonsense. That ol' gal was just too much horse for 'em, too big an' too smart. As for myself, I got so I admired her. But ever since then when I'm fixin' to get in a wagon, I always walk around and check that it's got all its nuts and cotter pins.

Mo said That's just how Mr. Brick is, he checks stuff out, an' he don't miss a thing. But I couldn't help it, I just had to set him straight. I said Nobody's got eyes in the back of their head. If you want a real lesson in what's going on around you, just watch your horse. All the while she's watching something, she might be listening to something else with her ears swiveling around, and at the same time she might be smelling a third thing coming this way on the wind. Her eyesight might not be as good as ours in the daylight, but her hearing and smelling are sharper than ours, and make all the difference. Plus she sees in the dark pretty good.

The boys yelped at that, then told us good night, and Eva tucked them in their new sleeping bags in their new tent, and came back over to the fire and said the boys both said their new stuff smells funny. But they agreed with me that you sure got some stories, Mr. Brick. Clint said That's a couple a hard ones for sure. Then I told 'em both I'd thought of one more that I held back tonight, that I wasn't sure the boys were ready for. Well then, why don't you try it out on us, Eva said for them both, so I did.

I told them about how my boyhood friend Larry had somehow got a horse that never wanted to be caught or ridden. He lived on a farm near us, and one of his uncles gave it to him because his own kids couldn't ride it, and he was tired of chasing it. Maybe Larry's uncle and cousins were just too impatient or scared around it to make friends. It's for sure he didn't have anyone around who knew much about horses, who might have shown him better ways of working with a shy or skitterish animal. But one afternoon while Larry was running around the barnyard trying to catch it, the horse ran into the garden, where the gate had been left open, and that horse backin' away from him kicked over a beehive, and the bees rushed out and stung it all over, till it looked like the poor horse had been wrapped in a splotchy gold rug round its back and belly, all up its neck, down its ears and face and nose. Before long the horse sagged down, gasping and wheezing, tried to shake and roll the bees off but was too weak. Larry told me he ran to find his dad and call the vet, but his father was off tilling some corn on the tractor and wouldn't call anyone, said he was tired of that damn horse forever costing him. So Larry went back to the horse, but was too scared of the bees to get close, and the horse died a few hours later, in the twilight just past sunset. Then the bees flew away in a swarm, ignoring the wreckage of the hive.

I said That story's always bothered me. I got to see that dead horse the next day. Don't recall that it ever had a name. But now I got a hard question for you--what do you think you'da done?

Eva answered first, said she'da called the vet right away, and not wasted time telling the dad. 'Cause Larry already knew what his dad thought. You gotta do what you do when there's a fire--you jump to it. Then she said While I was at it I'da also called the nearest bee-keeper around.

Then Clint said he'da got a brush and a water hose, and got the bees off the horse right away, if he could.

I said What about the bees stingin' you?

Clint said I was thinkin' of a hose with a nozzle, and a brush with a long handle. But to save him we'd have to work fast.

Eva said she didn't think we'd get in that kinda fix.

Clint said Why not?

'Cause thanks to Brick we're mostly thinkin' of the horses first. And we wouldn't leave the garden gate open. Or chase a horse.

What would you do if you wanted to ride?

I know what the boys would say. I'd have a little something in my pocket for it, and a rope. Then I'd just walk up, say hello and visit with it a little. Be in no hurry, an' see what works out. That horse might not a been as bad as he thought.

Then Eva sat quiet. Clint said he'd seen how bee-keepers work, with a smoker, and a veil and gloves and all. But horses are prob'ly just as scared of fire as bees are, so I like my answer best. To get the bees off the poor thing. Would a shop-vac work, or a leaf blower?

I said That's a good idea. But you'd need a good long extension cord. And if the machine's not big enough, you might just plug it up, and hafta stop and clean out all those angry bees.

At that point they both quieted down and looked at me. I said I been thinkin' about this forever. I didn't know so much back then, and wasn't there, though next day we talked it all over while I helped Larry dig the hole. That's all we talked about for hours. Then his dad brought the tractor and chain and drug the horse out, to where we could roll the poor thing in and shovel it under.

But years later I talked to the vet I still use, and she said it might have already been too late, no matter what you tried. A good strong hive at the peak of the summer season can hold 60 to 100,000 bees. If a hive gets attacked, the first thing the worker bees will do is go fill up on the nectar in the open combs that are still fermenting, that haven't been capped with wax yet. It's an emergency measure, in case they have to swarm and go make a new hive somewhere else, they'll have something to feed the babies. They get so full they can't bend their abdomen to stick the stinger in. That's why bee-keepers use smoke, they say it gentles the bees, but really the bees think the hive is on fire, and get themselves too full of nectar and honey, sometimes so full they can't fly. A bear can knock over a hive and eat the honey, because its fur is so thick an' long the bees can only get at a few places around its nose and eyes. Water is a good idea if you can get it there right away, and scraping away the stingers can lessen the poison in the horse's system. But the bees responded instantly, and if the horse couldn't get away, it might not stand a chance. If I'da been right there I'da given the horse all the Benadryl I had, that I carry in my saddlebag for insects and snakebites and such, since it sounds like the poor critter couldn't breathe, and died of anaphylactic shock. The vet lady said the best thing to do for the future if you have animals is put up an extra fence around the hives.

Why Don't Horses Laugh

If you're not around kids all the time you can forget how they grow and change, sometimes quick as popcorn or bubble gum popping, sometimes slow as a garter snake shedding last year's skin, a bit indignant if you never caught the new shine as she squirmed out of the dusty old one. Some days kids leave you scratching your head at where all that new might have come from, even when they're just repeating what you said when you thought they weren't listening.

So one fine spring day after school in third grade Mo dashed into the barn behind Ike and said Hey Mom, Mr. Brick: Why couldn't the pony sing? And when we looked up he said 'Cause she was a little hoarse.

Then he said I got a new white horse that I call Mayo. And sometimes Mayo neighs.

Then he said Why can't your head be 12 inches long? 'Cause then it'd be a foot.

With that he was off and running, rattling off jokes at his mom and Ike and me. Mo had always had a quick wit and a funny bone, but this was something else. What kind of key opens a banana? A monkey. What do you get from a cow in an earthquake? A milkshake. They came at us so fast for a while there the laughter swelled up and spilled over from one to the next till we could hardly catch our breath and stop laughing quick enough to hear the next one he fired at us. For Mo it was clearly a joy, a new power, and he already knew that first day not to laugh at his own jokes, keep a poker face, and give a little pause before he hit the punchline. But then sometimes he couldn't help ducking his head and letting a little smile leak past.

Eva and I had just taken a ride around the place, getting her some practice for taking longer rides with her two young ones, and the two mares we were currying didn't know what to make of this outburst. Beulah and Lady reared their heads back and rolled their eyes like it might be catching

--or something outrageous underfoot like a field mouse playing Tea for Two on harmonica.

Finally I got him to slow down and let us catch our breath. And say where he came by the jokes. And he said From our new teacher Miss Melanie Rawls, who is a really funny lady. She just started today, an' she's got bright red hair and a green dress and hundreds an' thousands a jokes, dozens an' millions, and 'splained to us how they work. She even showed us some of her secret tricks. The biggest one is you gotta have a surprise they can't see that's coming straight at 'em all the while. Then the surprise has to be something you get in an instant, that's sharp and tight and cracks like a whip.

I said Does she look funny when she's telling a joke?

No, she looks dead serious.

I said Like Lady does right now? He looked up at his favorite horse, and saw how she was watching him with what looked a lot like concern. He stepped close, rubbed her neck and patted her shoulder to let her know it was all right.

Why should a joke bother her?

Mo thought about it a minute. Said Maybe she just never learned how to laugh.

At which point his mother and brother looked at each other and grinned.

Then Mo said So why did the boy eat his homework?

I said I didn't know.

'Cause his dog didn't like excuses. We all laughed but the two mares still looked a little dubious, rearing up and tipping back their long heads.

I got one for you, Mo. What's the matter with these poor horses?

He said he didn't know. I said Guess. Then he said Maybe they don't know what a joke is.

Then I said Fine an' dandy. So why don't you tell that last joke again, and show them it's just a game we play, that means them no harm. Maybe they're just not used to all this laughin'.

Mo looked over at Lady, the horse he knew best, who'd lowered her head to study him, then back at me, then said Okay. So why did the boy eat his homework?

I pointed at Eva. She said 'Cause his teacher said it was a piece of cake. Then I pointed at Ike. He said 'Cause his horse wasn't hungry. Then I pointed at myself and said 'Cause his dog was a weed-eater. Then I pointed at Mo, and he said 'Cause it was covered with his favorite special sauce. Then we all looked at each other and laughed. But this time the two horses looked calm, like they knew the silliness wasn't catching, and would pass.

Later in the evening after dinner around the fire pit we talked some more about whether horses had a sense of humor. I said I didn't think they did, 'cause they were sincere and direct in everything they did. Unless they're sulking, 'cause they thought they'd been forgotten, or treated wrong. I thought when horses were babies they could really be funny, with their serious little faces, and sometimes seemed like they were trying to make us laugh. But then in a year or so they mostly outgrew their little play world, except with the closest of friends. They got to that awkward stage that lasted a year or two, where they were always too little or big for their britches. Besides, they didn't understand wordplay, and didn't know that many words anyhow. Mo said he guessed I was right, since he'd never seen a horse laugh, or a chicken either. I said I'd seen horses open their mouths and stick out their teeth and tongue, that looked like they might be trying to laugh but was prob'ly just a sneeze or hiccup or brain fart. If you called one horse by another horse's name he just thought you didn't mean him. And your horse knew if you were mad at him or not. Your tone of voice and body language said all a horse needed to know.

Mo asked if a dog could have a sense of humor, and Ike said he thought they did, or else they just have a happy dance that was the same to them as laughing, with their tongue hanging out, with their eyes wide and a big toothy grin, shaking from head to tail like they're trying to jump out of their skin. Anyhow, he said That's how our Melody used to do. And if they see you bein' happy, they just want to jump in the pile, roll around on the rug and lick your face to see what you been eating.

Clint thought Mo's jokes were great fun, and said he wished when he was a kid that jokes weren't so cruel. Mo said What do you mean, and he said Some kids told jokes about other kids' mamas, that seemed like they were just meant to start a fight, 'cause that was what usually happened. And then there were jokes about people's appearance that were plain heartless too, where nobody laughed unless they were trying to rub it in. I told Clint sometimes I just tried to play deaf around school but that never worked for long. Clint told about one family in his school that had head lice one winter, and all their heads were shaved. It wasn't so bad for the boys, but the girls just hated it, and got teased for wearing stocking caps. The boys would run past them and snatch off their caps, and shout Hey, Baldy--what'cha hiding there?

Mo didn't know what lice were, so Eva explained they were also called bedbugs, that liked to get in the roots of the hair in a person's scalp, and made you itch somethin' awful, and how they were specially hard to get rid of, when little kids might take naps together, or share beds. She said The first time I saw a girl who'd had her head shaved, who'd had beautiful long curly hair, someone whispered she must be dying of a brain tumor, and I cried. But let's get back to jokes.

Clint told a joke I'd told him while he was building their house, about the lightning-rod salesman and the farmer who was raising three-legged chickens. The boys didn't know what a lightning-rod salesman was, but they sure got the punchline. Mo said he was going to tell that one to Miss Melanie Rawls tomorrow first thing, if we thought it was okay.

I said I thought that would be a fine one to tell in class. All your jokes are plenty good for humans, and sure do tickle me. Maybe horses don't have a sense of humor because they don't need one. They have a herd mind that lets them all think together, that humans don't do so much, and could probably use more of, but seem to like goin' their own way, that leaves them feeling superior. We use humor to get rid of tension, and deal with things we don't understand and can't change, that would bother us other-wise. But horses are prey animals, naturally quiet because they need to hear and smell and see predators coming in time to hide or run away. Laughter wasn't an option since it would just call attention to them and what they thought of a world that didn't always make sense, that might bite them for ignoring. It's also worth noticing how closely horses watch their riders, all the while pretending not to. Horses study their surroundings and know their world pretty well, except for some of the humans they're around, who keep surprising them, and not always in good ways.

Then just as Eva was going to take the boys in to bed, I thought of something else. So I asked them if jokes are so fun, why weren't we all born laughing? Eva said, That's easy, because it hurts to be born--most of us get squeezed pretty hard. So babies have to learn, and it takes months, sometimes a year or more for us to learn to laugh, even though most of us have people laughing all around. Then I told them how I met a Navaho woman years back over breakfast in a fry-bread shack in Chinle, Arizona. We got to talking about her three small well-mannered children who were digging in the dirt in the shade outside while she cooked in the little cafe with only a counter and three tables. Her three little children all smiled wide and had the same tiny chuckle she had. She told me her people had a custom, that the first grownup who got the new baby to laugh--and no fair tickling-- got to host a party that she said was welcome to the world. Everybody in the community would be invited, because a new baby can't have too many aunties and uncles and friends, and there would be sweet and salty gifts from the baby for all the party-goers, to season the living, and there would be singing and dancing and storytelling where the baby would be passed around and made the center of everything, all day and on into the night.

When I was done and looked up, Mo was standing close, looking at me like Lady had been looking at him in the barn. I said What?

He said I was waiting for it to be funny. I said it wasn't meant to be. This Navaho lady Lucy told me laughing was just the sign the little one was ready to enter this world that is our only home. At the end she said you might not believe it, but the party would mostly be quiet and move in slow motion, even the singing and dancing, so as not to startle the little one. And those were the best parties, since the grownups mostly behaved, and the little one would fall asleep in someone's arms and be gently handed back to her mother as if a gift from us all.

The Roundup You Don't Forget

That next spring the boys got to herd cattle for the first time. We spent a few days after school practicing with lariats on fence posts and other stuff. The handlebars of a wheelbarrow tipped up with its wheel in a rut made a pretty fair imitation of the feet of a calf, or the horns of a full-grown cow, that would sit still long enough to drop a loop on. We also sawed out a wooden cow head with bike handlebar horns and screwed it onto the end of an old sawhorse that we put on wheels, with a line to pull it around like a wobbly toy. The boys were trying hard, but weren't quite up to roping just yet, especially not from the saddle. The rawhide and nylon lariats I had around the place turned out to be way too heavy. So we picked up some cotton clothesline from the hardware store that would be lighter to toss, plus a couple of straw cowboy hats for the roundup. I meant to let them have some fun and feel a little success that might come in handy later on.

Then on Saturday we talked a little about herding cattle, how to be easy and calm, steer from behind and either side, give them room and time to decide to do what we wanted. There were only a few tricks, like pressing them from behind on the side where we wanted them to turn around us. The biggest thing was to stay in contact, keep as close as they'd let you, and be in no hurry. Then we put on our hats, saddled up and left the ropes behind, to ride around the big open pasture to the far fence line. There was one change--I told Ike I needed to work Beulah today, and he should ride Lucky while Mo rode Lady. At the far end of the big pasture we turned around, then swept the cattle quietly and gently before us. I rode drag on Beulah, zigzagging a little back and forth, with one of the boys halfway back on either side. The horses were calm, and didn't mind workin' cattle. As for the cattle, we didn't press 'em much, and they moved just fine. It took us a couple hours to gather up all the cattle on that two square miles, and herd them into the big corral, where we'd sort the breeding stock from the new calves. The hard part would be cutting out calves from their attentive, indignant mamas, which happened Sunday afternoon. Finally on Monday we would run the new little ones through the squeeze gate for branding, castration and shots, though for now I was planning to leave the boys out of that.

The real surprise at this roundup was how the boys got to see Beulah with new eyes. She'd always been a pretty fair cutting horse and had just gotten more savvy with time, but the boys hadn't seen any cutting work until now, separating calves from their mamas out in the pasture or in the big corral. I laid out the situation for them, described where we wanted the cows and calves to be. After thinking about it for a few minutes, Ike said How about if we tackle the job as a team and all work one gate at a time? I said Fine. What if one of you just stay behind the gate and the other out of the way up on the rail so you don't spook 'em. Then we got right to it. Gate-keeping was a job they did promptly and well, improvising as we went along. Beulah and I would peel off a calf from its mama, steer the little one toward the gate, then turn and block mama's way, while Mo would hop down from his perch on the rail, get behind the calf and steer it in with some fancy cartoon footwork, while Ike crouched behind the gate, set to swing it wide then slam it shut. The surprise was how they made kind of a game of it, practically a dance, as they whistled and hooted and pointed to signal each other what to do. The calves were quick and unpredictable, but fancy footwork and all, the boys were quicker and at least as baffling to the calves as any horse could be. When one cow got past me, both boys had to bluff the mama off as she came huffing after her little one. They did a tight little dance round and round each other right up to the gate, then shoved the calf through as the horse and I arrived to cut off mama. Beulah was persistent and worked the calves with her sweet, abrupt moves. By the end hardly a calf got past either her or the boys. Then we herded all the mamas and older cattle into their own pen. By the time we were done, we were whistling and calling and waving just like old-time cowboys.

I was proud of them and said so. The smallest of those calves easily outweighed either of the boys. But Ike and Mo had ridden their horses well, and on foot were deft and unafraid. On the ground they took their gatekeeper job seriously, but were sure-footed and confident enough to be playful. And it didn't hurt that they knew each other's moves so well the teamwork was a breeze. Of course when their dad got home we got to hear about the day all over from the top, with Beulah's moves bluffing the cows, and the dance moves with the calves acted out in the firelight.

Ike finally turned and asked me Do you think Beulah likes cutting cows?

Yes, I think she does, since she caught on so fast and does it so well. She tricks and fakes 'em, and makes 'em do what she wants. And at the same time she likes pleasing us.

I'd arranged for Reynaldo and Clyde to give me a hand the next day, a Monday, with branding, castrating, tags and shots and the rest, while the boys were at school. My two old hands were still living in the bunk-house, working odd jobs on some neighboring farms and ranches. Though I hadn't had steady work for them since the drought had shut us down, I gave 'em a few hours here and there, haying, and moving and doctoring the stock. I'd bought and bred a couple batches of heifers with some of the money from those lots I'd sold, trying to build the herd up, and get the Pipestone back on its feet. We'd counted eighteen healthy new calves this spring, and thirty heifers and cows to be bred soon for the following spring. It was nothing like years past, but was better than I had any right to expect. As the old-timers used to say doctoring sick animals, it looked like I was back on my feed, and starting to take an interest.

That Monday was a busy day, with ten bull calves to be fixed, then branding and shots for all eighteen. I had a pretty good squeeze-gate with a calf table, that saved a lot of the wrestling and backache when an animal had to be doctored. We'd just catch the calf in the gate, lay it down on its side, get a couple lines on its feet and stretch it out.

When the boys stepped off the bus that afternoon, they ran straight over to see how things were going. We had been hoping to have all the mess cleaned up, but were still carrying the picnic table and cooler of medicines back to the barn when they scrambled up onto the rail to look in at the calves. But there was still a bucket with bloody rags in it inside the barn door, that Ike couldn't help but spot. He stopped there, looked up at me and said Do they hurt much? I said It's not so bad. Branding prob'ly hurts more and lasts longer. Just somethin' we gotta do. You know about steers, that we fatten for market. He said, They're bulls, ain't they. Yes, I said, Young bulls, extra bulls. Usually we only need one on the place. Even one at a time can turn into a handful. Then Ike turned away, looked out at the empty pasture, and at the near pen full of lowing and bellowing cattle. He said, You know, we're not babies.

I said, Yeah, I know. And you worked great yesterday. But we don't want to be in an all-fired hurry till you get a little more size to you, so you don't get hurt. And if we can help it, we don't wanna to be givin' you boys any nightmares. Okay?

I didn't want to crowd him any. He turned away, knuckled an eye, then slowly turned back to me. And said Okay. Then I said We got one more chore to do with the calves before we go in. I saw Eva walking out toward Mo and waved them over.

In their pen the calves were still bawling, and I could hardly blame 'em. They were sore from the doctoring, and missing their mamas who were lowing off in the distance, in a far pen with the rest of the cattle. Ike was showing Mo the orange antiseptic spray on some of the calves' bellies. I told the boys we needed to find the three smallest ones, that were bred late and born a month after the others, that were still too young to wean. Pretty soon we located them, and I said We need to keep a close eye on these three, and probably ought to put 'em right back in with their mamas. Mo said What for? that just got a laugh from Ike. Eva said They need their dinner. Then he said So how we gonna catch 'em? I said Why don't you boys go get your lassos--and bring mine off my saddle. We'll just drop a loop over 'em, and walk 'em over to the other pen, and let their mamas pick 'em out. Who would know better than they do whose is whose? Mo said How can they tell? Ike said Remember the one we saw just getting born? Her mama licked her all over. She must know what her own baby tastes like. And with that the boys raced off to the barn to find their ropes, while Eva choked back a laugh, snuck a finger under my elbow and poked me. She said Lucky all three of those little ones turned out to be girls. I'm starting to see they're bound to learn it all around here, especially stuff there's no hiding anyhow.

While the boys were getting their lassos I needed one more thing, and headed to the house with Eva in tow. There I got a clean bucket, poured a quart of milk in it, and we went out to meet the boys back at the pen.

Each of the boys hit their calf on the first toss, so of course I was bound to miss mine. But as I suspected, the calves were pretty squirrelly and a handful for the boys, fighting the rope till we stuck that milk under their noses and gave them all a taste, then we got Eva holding the bucket to lead us over to the other gate. With their mamas right there, crowding the gate and shoving their noses through, we shouldered 'em back and let the little ones in, where their mamas knew whose was whose and what to do, and it seemed like all at once the noise and commotion died down, and our work was done.

Taken for a Spin

One afternoon Ike asked me how old I was when I first rode a horse. We were rocking on the front porch in the shade, with a glass of iced tea, while Mo was off helping his mother plant some sunflower seeds in the yard for later, for the winter birds. I said I couldn't rightly say where or when I first rode by myself, but recall someone handing me up high to someone else, who set me in front of him on a saddle, set my little hands on the horn and said Hold on tight. It was my father who'd handed me up, then stepped on his own horse, and my grandfather who went riding off with me around a wide field full of cattle, so wide there seemed like no fences at all. It was noisy and smelly, dusty and bright. Grampa had on a big white hat, and his horse was black, with white feet and a white blaze down his face. His big hand and arm were around my middle, so I felt safe, though after a little while I reached out to grab the horse's mane. With his hair in my grip I could feel the horse moving, his legs lifting and his neck reaching out as we loped along in and out of the cattle. Grampa was talking to me, saying "cow" and "horse" and "calf," familiar words, though he said some other things I had no clue what they meant. I couldn't talk much yet, but somehow knew he was talking about all this, what was going on in this huge open grassy place, under the sun in a deep blue sky streaked with a few high-blown clouds. From up there in the saddle it was all familiar and friendly, a ride as easy as this old rocking chair.

Then we stopped, and my father on his horse eased up next to us. The two of them talked awhile, and I could feel my grandfather's voice as if it was rumbling inside a me, shaking me, my ear up against him as he spoke. Then he lifted me to my feet and held me close as he leaned back and turned his horse all the way round, so I got to see it all. The horse put his front feet in the air. And all I could see was cattle and horses, grass and sun and them happy eating and frolicking. All their switching tails. Then he stopped spinning, set the horse back down, then leaned over and handed

97

me back to my father, who nudged his horse close and took me.

That's not just my first horse ride, that's my first memory. I guess like old farmers say, the apple don't fall far from the tree.

Did they do that with all their kids?

I couldn't say. I never saw that done with anyone else.

What do you suppose your grampa was saying to you?

I laughed, and said Maybe some day, little man, all this will be yours. Of course, where the story ends is right where the daydreams get going. When you're young, sometimes it's hard to know what's really going on in grownups' heads. Before you can talk you're a lot like a horse, where all you know is the tone of their voice, and the tastes and smells of the natural world. You guess from the way they stand and what they're looking at, what they're studyin' an' fixin' to do next. But sometimes we get blind-sided. Sometimes at just the wrong minute our back is turned, and we miss something that would have explained the whole thing. So what do we really know? I do know that old man was younger than I am now, and the way he turned that horse round and round was like we were on a mountain top, where he could show me the world. That little spin he took says it all--says he was a real horseman, had a good horse, and brought something to show-and-tell that was out of the ordinary, that said the wide-open spaces we sat in the middle of, for him seemed to live and breathe at the heart of every-thing.

Then I stopped a second, and warned Ike not to believe everything old folks like me might say. Sometimes all we had was snatches of stuff that had happened, that somehow got stitched up or hammered into a story, that we got to like tellin' so well we half-believed it ourselves. I told him part of most every story is a little too good or too bad to be true, since memory is a fickle thing, like dreams that come at you all at once, and all wrong, that we shuffle up in the telling to help it make sense. And sometimes without even knowing we're doing it, we hide the ugliest or most baffling parts from ourselves.

After dark around the Mosley's firepit later that night, when the boys came out in their pajamas to say good night, Ike asked if I'd tell his parents and brother my first memory. And I said How about when we have more time, 'cause I want to hear all your first memories too, every one's. So that's what we did the next night, after we'd just cut into our first peach pie, that I'd picked then peeled, sliced and baked from that tree we'd planted the day I first met the boys several springs ago.

I said They say time flies, but never said it might turn out this tasty. After we'd lined our innards with pie and vanilla ice cream, Ike reminded us all what he wanted to hear.

His dad Clint stood up, and said his earliest memory was when he was four, when he was in church with his parents. It was during the sermon, that was loud and long and way over his head. He was feeling impatient, and trapped, and started kicking the seat in front of him, that bothered the big bald man sitting there, who turned around and glared, not just at him but at his mom and dad. Then his mother leaned down, yanked his arm and whispered Stop kickin' the seat--God won't like it. He considered just exactly what she'd said, not "don't" but "won't." Like God wouldn't know till she told him--like he spent all his time listening to parents and no time watching kids. Clint said he started to think that was what grownups' prayers must be like, all just telling on each other. And he said That's right when I started not believing their stories about an invisible old God who knew everything and judged it all, then sent you to heaven or hell.

Eva said she'd like to go next, and stood up. She said her first memory was a little older, the summer she turned five, when she was staying with her mom's friends. She didn't know it at the time, but that was when her mama had another baby, her little brother Joey, right before her father died in a car wreck. The couple she was staying with didn't have any kids. The woman Marie was a school nurse who was off for the summer, and her husband Nathan had what they called a truck garden, farming a few acres. On the porch they had a beautiful gong, mostly made out of bronze and brass. The gong part was a big round dish with an Indian chief in a feather headdress scratched deep in the face of it, and it was hanging from an elk or moose antler that was attached to a real turtle shell on the bottom, with a turtle's head and feet and tail sticking out, all made of brass. Marie used this gong to call Nathan in from the fields and the barn for his meals. It made a loud and beautiful sound when you hit it with the special stick with a deer-skin-covered ball on one end.

When she'd first got there she'd loved that Indian gong, and she went out on the porch and rang it a hundred times the first day. But then on the second morning Marie told her that Nathan had kept hearing it and got confused, thinking she wanted him or needed him when she didn't. So she made a deal with Eva that she could ring it for lunch and dinner, as loud as she wanted, if she didn't ring it any other times. She'd said When I have lunch and dinner fixed, I'll tell you, so you can go ring the gong. In her excitement Eva thought maybe Marie was afraid she'd wear out the gong, or break it, but it seemed so sturdy. Maybe she was afraid it would wear out her ears. But Eva couldn't get enough of that beautiful sound. She'd never heard anything like it. So for several days Eva said she tried to be good, and just ring it when Marie told her she could.

But that first weekend when Marie needed to go to the store for groceries, Eva didn't want to go. Marie said she could stay home if she promised to be good, and go get Nathan if she needed anything. But as soon as Marie was out the driveway in the car, Eva lifted the gong down from the hutch on the porch where it stood, dragged it inside and hefted it onto the rug. It was very heavy, and hard to lift, but she wanted to ring it so bad she said she couldn't help it. She said It was the first time I'd ever disobeyed a grownup about anything. Then she went around the house and closed all the windows and doors, so nobody outside would hear. Finally she sat there on the floor and rang it as hard and loud and long as she could, till she was exhausted. It made the plates and teacups and glasses ring in Marie's china cupboard. It rattled the window panes.

Then all at once there was Nathan standing in the open door, holding his engineer cap in his hand. She was so frightened she dropped the stick. He was looking right at her, but he didn't look mad. He said I thought it was a fire alarm, from somewhere miles away. I came in to call the volun-teers and see if they needed a hand. But now I can see where the fire is. And he smiled. Then he said Why don't you go ahead and ring it another couple hundred times, then I'll put it back up on the hutch outside. That's an awful heavy thing, and we'd hate for you to drop it on your toes. Maybe what we should do is let you ring it whenever Marie is gone shopping, and just keep it a secret. You know, you should hear how she does it sometimes, so gentle seems like she's whispering right in my ear. She only bangs it that hard when she's mad at me, and wants me to know it for sure.

Then Eva looked around at us and sat down, and Ike stepped into the firelight. He said I don't even know for sure if this is my first memory, but in time maybe I'll find out if there's anything else back there that's ever grabbed me more. It's about our dog, Mr. Brick. She was just a mutt, but we liked her. That morning Melody got out, slipped through the door that wasn't quite shut and got away, I didn't think, I just ran after her. I wondered why she even wanted to get out, but since then I've seen how Mo and I just want to get out in the open sometimes and run, just run. 'Specially right after school. But this time I stomped my foot and clapped my hands, called Melody and said Come! But she wouldn't, she pretended she didn't hear me and kept running. I've seen the horses do that, let themselves get excited and not calm down till they get tired of running, then they stop and look around like they just woke up in this strange place. It's been three years now, but I keep seeing it over and over in my mind. How she ran between the cars and got hit by that lady just driving a little too fast in her new yellow car. The next car almost hit me when I stopped and bent down. There was Melody whimpering and looking up at me, but she couldn't move. I petted her but then she just started shaking. Then before anybody could do a thing, she quit looking out through her eyes, and was gone. There was nothing in her moving her any more. For a long time I said it was someone else who must have let her out, but it was me. I was the last one to come in that door, and I didn't remember to close it. And for that I am sorry. And I will never forget.

When Ike was done, he sat down next to his folks. Anyone could see he felt terrible, but had remembered and said what he had to. Then Mo got up and stepped close to the fire. He said I don't know if I seen enough yet to know it was my first, either, but I sure remember that first day when we got to ride with Dad and Mom in his truck out here to the place where he was building us a new house. It was such a nice day we got to ride in the back, if we sat down and held on and didn't bounce outa there. When we got here I couldn't even figure out what it was. There was a hole in the ground where the house was gonna be, that had concrete in the bottom and sides like a swimming pool. There were some heavy boards stood up on their edge over that, and sheets of plywood nailed down that showed where the floor was gonna be. But there was no way to tell how tall it might get, no walls and no roof, and there was no yard yet, nothing but red dirt and yellow dirt. But then there was this new fence, with grass on the other side, and a couple of horses and a couple of cows that had some baby cows. And I said hello and waved, and they came close to see what we were up to. So Ike and me pulled some grass and reached through the fence to feed 'em, and they were all friendly and seemed glad to see us, even though we didn't hardly have a house here or anything yet. Then we looked up and saw Mr. Brick way over by his house, so I went and asked Mom if we could go over and see what he was doing. She said yes, if you watch and don't step in any cow pies, and mind your manners and don't bother him. So we ducked through the fence, and walked across the field to where there was a gate, and we went through and closed it, and saw he was digging a hole. So we watched him a while, and he asked us our names, and told us his, and said he could use some help holding this little peach tree straight. And it wasn't long before I wondered why I was so happy, watching him fill in that hole, and thought it must be because this was the first day of our whole new life. And some time there might even be peaches that I didn't even know since I'd never tasted one yet 'cause I was scared they were fuzzy. But they sure turned out to be good.

Then Mo looked around, and everyone clapped, which made him beam like he'd just found a shiny brandnew quarter in the dirt.

Then Ike reminded me they had to hear my story, so I told about being a little one in my grandfather's lap, and him turning his big black horse around in the sun with me holding onto his mane. I thought it was probably better told on the porch late in the day in an old rockin' chair, facing the night out ahead, but they all hushed when it was done, though there was no more to it than any of the others we'd heard, maybe less. But that's how it is with your life, that feels best surrounded and in touch with all those other lives. So maybe we're just herd animals too. And there we all sat quiet and poked at the fire till Eva told the boys it was time for bed. Then I got up myself, and told 'em all to sleep tight, and don't let the bedbugs bite, and headed in.

A Horse of a Different Color

That spring I finally had a decent excuse to reconnect with my father. I needed a couple of horses so I could take the Mosleys all back-country camping together, and when I called him, he said Just come pick out a couple from the posse--you know, the chocolate ones. We're feedin' too many a them as it is. "The posse" was code he and Grampa had used for the plain brown horses none of their dude clientele cared to ride. As if a horse were a fashion statement or accessory. So Dad was still on the lookout for alternatives--appaloosas, paints, palominos, red-roans with white stockings, blue roans dappled with moonlight, duns with black legs, manes and tails -- anything striking, exotic. So we named a day, and I hitched up the fifth wheel trailer to the truck and paid the old Moon-Dog Ranch a visit. It was a couple-hour drive and then some, but he was out on the porch waiting, so we sat there and had coffee, though it was sneakin' up on ten in the morning. I was tryin' not to put him out any, just behave.

We commiserated some about Grampa, though he'd made it to 95 and been gone eight years now, since before the big drought. But there I was sittin' in his chair, a match to the one Dad was ridin', and reminders of the bossman weren't far to seek. I didn't really want to look around, just get this chocolate horse business done. He even had somethin' new I hadn't heard. You know what the old man's dying words were? I shook my head. "I know that bill's around somewhere." That got us to grin and commiserate, how he was the same cussed know-it-all right to the end, sweatin' the small stuff. We chatted a little, but I couldn't miss noticing here was my dad in his old everyday hat and boots, set to look over some horses. So when my mug was empty I shook it out and eased up. And said Dad, you wanta go out and show me some horses? I don't want to go stealin' none a your favorites. Which he gave a small laugh, then responded Not likely.

This horse-picking didn't need to be work, but you wanted your wits about you. I skipped back to get a few things from the truck--a lasso, a couple of halters and lead ropes, and a few apples in a paper sack. Then we hobbled out and let ourselves into the big corral. But when we got there Dad seemed to have forgotten all he and Grampa had once preached about picking a horse. The two of them used to repeat each other's lines, and laugh in unison, as if savoring punchlines to old jokes that needed retelling in a world fulla idjits. It's like they both had the same little homemade Horseman's Bible in their heads, where either or both could close their eyes and rattle off a quote. Like "Lead your new horse round a little, and watch how he picks up and puts down his feet. Speed up and slow a couple times, then call out Whoa. Then back him up. If he moves well, listen to how he breathes. If you're still serious, go get someone else to lead him a few minutes while you watch. If he's not cow-hocked or pigeon-toed, with no paddlin' or dishin', no hitch or limp or lameness, nothin' wrong with his wind, mount up and sit him. Is his head up, waitin' the sign to go? If not, pass him by."

I'd heard them go through this litany hundreds of times, that included teeth and feet, ears and endless details of conformation, down to shapes and sizes of heads, and never once did they mention the color of a horse. As far as they'd been concerned when I grew up, cowboys might as well been color-blind.

When we waded in, Dad said You wanta ride some? I said First let's just see what we got. The horses slowly swirled around us, and for the moment seemed color-blind themselves. But then I noticed most of the chocolate ones were gathered in a patch of shade near the barn, with a few pretty ones hiding in among the plain and sensible ones. So that's where I headed, and Dad stomped along behind. A few of the older ones looked familiar, but I was looking for young blood that might keep awhile. When I got close I shuffled my feet and feinted as if to chase the posse a little to one side, watching for which ones didn't stumble, freak or balk, who'd have gotten away if I were a cougar. Only three would have made it for sure.

Dad had already wondered off to find a hand or two that might know their way around the stock, while I just eased around among the brown horses and kept looking 'em over. When I saw one I liked, I got an apple out of the bag and clicked my tongue, and he looked up and walked over to see was I givin' free samples. Then while he worked on the apple I slid a loop over his head, but waited till he was done, then walked him up and down a little to see how he did. In a few minutes Dad was back at my elbow. When I said How about this one, he said Wouldn't you know you'd pick one I don't know a thing about. 'Course, all these lunkheads look alike. He turned to one of the hands in a big brown hat with a tall triple-dented crown, and said Mayberry? You know this one? Mayberry lifted his lid and scratched his head, then said That's Nokey, used to be Teddy Broom's steady horse, till he moved on. Nobody's rode him since early last year, but he's a good 'un. Mayberry caught my rope, pulled Nokey's head close, caught his chin, pulled back his lips and looked over his teeth. Then said He looks to be six or seven. When I asked what the name meant, Mayberry said Teddy was forever losin' the key to his pickup, an' said that's what he liked about horses. Nokey.

I stepped close, put a halter on Nokey, petted him a little and tied him up near the front gate. Dad had spotted another couple of brown horses for me to look at, but I noticed the mare was missing a rear shoe, so we looked at the other, another young gelding that Mayberry said was sad-dle-broke but had mostly been used for back-country excursions, packing grub and tents and the like. He had acquired the name of Cicero, on ac-count of how he held up his head like a noble Roman. I gave him an apple, admired his looks, and asked Mayberry if we could get the loan of a bridle and saddle and blanket for a couple minutes. While he went to get the gear I put the other halter and lead on Cicero, and tied him alongside Nokey. They were a likely pair, that standing together looked like they shared some blood. They might have been overlooked here, but should fit in where the horses got work, and didn't have such a herd to hide in.

When Mayberry got back, I gave Nokey another apple, picked up and looked at his feet while he ate it, then when he was done saddled and bridled him. I asked Dad if he'd watch to see was there anything to worry about. I figured to ride him around, then stir him up a little, run him to see if anything else showed. Dad nodded and grinned. Then I talked to Nokey a little, stroked his shoulder and neck, and told him what I was gonna do, then stepped up. Nokey shook his head like he had a bee in his ear and crow-hopped to one side, but I kept his head up and held my seat till he settled, then turned and rode him out past the big house maybe half a mile at a nice easy lope, then stopped, turned him a little this way and that, eased into the field and looped around a while, then spun him toward the road, dug my heels into him and let him run. I was a little surprised but gratified at how fast he moved out, down the gravel road straight as an arrow. That Teddy Broom musta been a go-getter, at least not fat and lazy, When I pulled up, Dad and Mayberry walked over as I stepped down. I asked if they saw anything, and Dad said You're goin' to the races on that one. Looks to be straight an' true, nothin' odd about him. How's he feel?

I said He's sure got his feet under him. Feels like I could run him all day. Mayberry talked a little about how that horse really stretches his neck out, like he's fixin' to get somewhere quick.

With that I handed Mayberry the reins, loosened Nokey's cinch and pulled the saddle off him. I put my lasso back around his neck, took his bridle off, and buckled the halter back on. Then I looked over at Dad and said this one's a keeper for sure.

Then in short order I heaved the rig onto Cicero, and let him have another apple, since he mighta been watchin' and countin'. Then I fed him the bit, and stepped up in the saddle, and headed him out onto the road. I turned into a field maybe a mile on and ran some tight figure-eights where they musta baled some late hay in the fall. This was a little younger horse who'd need to get used to a rider, green and skittish but quick, and he had no bad habits to speak of.

Then I put my heels to him, sent him on a tear, and before we knew it I was back at the big corral, where a huge cloud of dust caught up with me. I stepped down and tossed a loop over his head, then got the saddle and bridle off.

I told Dad, I think we're about done here. I can't even tell you which one is faster without a stopwatch, and both are solid, all horse, no complaints. So how's about eight hundred apiece for the two of them? He looked at me, shook his head and said That's not how you was taught to make a deal. You need to pick a little something to badmouth an' bring the price down.

Nosir. If you want to keep either or both of these, just say the word. In which case I'll keep lookin'. Otherwise I brought cash money. I got some good people going to ride with me, and we need solid horses. I'd feel better if they wasn't on loan, in case anything was to go wrong.

He looked me square in the eye. I watched, then said Eight hundred apiece might be a little light. I could maybe make it nine.

Hush, he said. You're no businessman. But I always knew you're the real horseman of the outfit.

And with that I stuffed the money in his shirt pocket, shook his big hard hand, and loaded these two plain brown ponies in the back. But then thought of one more chore--and went back to the big corral to rope that chocolate mare with the missing shoe, pen her and leave word with Dad so Mayberry would know where to find her. Then I turned the rig around in their big gravel yard, waved up at the old man in the shade, and headed home.

When I drove in, the boys ran over to see what I'd got, and were tickled when I said the pair of horses we got were pure chocolate. For the next week we worked the horses and checked the gear to get ready. Renaldo and Clyde had lent me their saddles, that all we had to do was oil up and shine the dust off. It was getting toward the end of March, and we wanted to go now, before the weather got hot, and were going to get the boys a week out of school. I put the two brown geldings in the same box stall, apart from the other horses till we could ride 'em enough to be agreeable. I explained to Ike and Mo, and they were really excited to have these two new horses for their folks. We had only one problem--at first no one but me could tell Nokey and Cicero apart. I took turns ridin' 'em both for the first three days to wear the rough off 'em, and to me Nokey had a shade darker mane and tail, and his eyes were a bit wider apart. The two of 'em held their heads up just the same, which made me suspect they'd had the same sire, though I'd have to talk to Dad about that. But I didn't give the Mosleys any clues about which was which. It was better if everyone was lookin' close, and findin' for themselves what made the difference. It was Eva and little Mo who could first tell 'em apart. Mo said Nokey had longer eyelashes and a brighter tail in the light. Eva said Nokey liked to snort when he was startled, and Cicero didn't. She said Cicero was a shade taller at the withers, and had slightly bigger front feet. I got them to repeat all that one evening, so maybe Ike and his dad Clint would look closer.

The one trouble we had right away was Cicero and Lucky started nippin' at each other, so I kept 'em apart and told the boys to keep an eye on 'em, 'cause we didn't want trouble. They were the youngest horses, both geldings, and I think Lucky might be a little younger, feeling the need to stand up for himself.

After a couple days we started Eva off ridin' Nokey, with the boys on Beulah and Lady, like they were used to. We had Eva give her horse a few treats, and handle him, pick up his feet like I'd been doing every day, and curry him. Then when Clint got home from work, he did the same with Cicero. Out in the pasture we'd ride a few loops round the whole place in the twilight, and let the horses get used to following each other, with us deciding who would go first, and changing often enough that the horses knew to do what we wanted. I did notice that as the light faded, Beulah would always step to the front, and the others let her, since she was older, and more confident. I had decided to try feeding Cicero and Lucky next to each other, in adjoining stalls, sometimes feeding one first, sometimes the other. I'd always give 'em treats together, when they were settled and paying attention. But they still seemed to want to mix it up, at least give each other the eye, so the last couple days I put each of them in with one of the two mares that were friendly to small boys and long on good sense.

We didn't have a spare animal to pack supplies, so I had to figure the cooking and eating close. I went through the kitchen, picked out one big aluminum skillet with a lid, a four quart aluminum pressure cooker, a mixing bowl, a coffee pot, a folding plastic water jug and a folding grill. Then I got out the bathroom scales, sorted the groceries and gear into four sacks, and tied two together to sling over each of our pommels. The hard part was making sure the pots and gear balanced, and got packed so they didn't clang together and bother the horses. We needed a rain slicker, a canteen and a flashlight apiece, and I packed a light 4-man tent we could all squeeze into, should the weather take a turn for the worse. We had a couple sacks of horse feed with five nose-bags. And in the horse trailer I had packed two burlap bags of firewood and charcoal, and a couple bales of hay we'd feed on either end. What meat we had was frozen and bubble-wrapped, and the eggs all fit in the pressure cooker wrapped in tissue paper with the lid locked down. I planned on letting the boys carry firewood and horse feed, and lettin' Clint and me haul the more breakable stuff.

With the bugs worked out as good as they'd likely get, we were set to leave well before daylight. Clint was going to follow my rig in his pickup, and the boys took turns riding with me for more room. We were heading south under a pale sliver of moon for Big Bend Ranch State Park along the Rio Grande, which would be quite a haul, near 500 miles. In fact, it took us all of a long day to get there, with stops for meals and potty breaks, stretching the horses and whatnot. We got into the park and to the first campsite I'd reserved just at dark, so we unloaded the horses into a corral that came with the campsite, tossed out half a bale from the trailer, fed and watered them, then set out a couple lanterns, got a fire going and ourselves settled in for late supper. I chopped up some polish sausage and potatoes, carrots and onions in the pressure cooker, poured in a cup of the boxed red wine along with salt and pepper and spices, and dug out some bowls and spoons. All we needed was biscuits, but it was gettin' late so this would have to do. The boys went around and propped up the saddles like I'd showed 'em, with the horns and pommels down, and checked to see that those two young horses weren't fighting.

Then we ate, and when we were about done I handed Clint and Eva a couple little paper bags from Bits & Spurs, a Western novelty store in town I'd been favoring. They were pudgy chocolate ponies for dessert. We all shared a nibble, and licked our fingers while we laughed.

Then we rolled out the bags, brushed our teeth, crawled in and called it a night.

Next morning in the lavender blue-gray dawn I tumbled out and put my boots on, then eased over to check on the horses, while the gang was still in dreamland. The horses looked good, and nickered to see me, so I tossed 'em some hay and topped up their water. Having the herd all in together seemed to have Cicero and Lucky on their best behavior. I slid inside the gate to look 'em over, but they all seemed fine. They knew this was a new place, but we were goin' somewhere else, so they were eager to get moving.

Hey, Mr. Brick, whatcha lookin' for? It was Ike, sitting barefoot on the top rail.

I said, Just feedin' the horses, and checkin' their shoes. You wanta get the shoe bag with my hammer in it, from my saddlebag? And get your boots on, but remember to shake 'em out first, 'cause there's snakes.

Sure thing. He hopped down and skipped to my saddle, then came back with the canvas bag that held my ferrier's tools and extra nails and shoes. I went over the horses and clinched down a few nails while I was thinking about it, though it hadn't been a week since I'd last checked.

Then it was time to boil water, make breakfast and get set to travel. I got the fire going, and asked Ike to go fill the coffee pot, and the pile of canteens. Then I mixed up some pancake batter, got out the butter and syrup, and slid the big pan on the grate. The sizzle of pancakes musta been music to these poor campers' ears, as they slowly rolled out and sat up.

There were a few other campers about, with outhouses nearby, but we were already off in a little world of our own. While we ate I described the plan, and passed around the maps and brochures with details and pictures of the park. A five-day loop, with campsites and corrals set out at regular intervals, most with water but one dry. We'd have to climb several mountain trails, but mostly we'd be riding over desert floor in early spring, with sparse vegetation, though out among the sage and cactus I'd already seen a few flowers.

It took a little while the first time to get ourselves set up to go, but we managed it. Clint and I saddled and bridled the horses, and tied them along the rail inside the corral. Then we rolled all the sleeping bags inside rain slickers and tied them on behind each rider's saddle. After that we tied the pairs of bags with food onto our horses, and the horse feed and a little hay in a couple of bags onto Mo's Lady, and a pair with firewood and charcoal onto Ike's Beulah. That left the tent and the sack of cooking tools and supplies for Eva's Nokey. As we mounted up I pointed to each horse and said what they were carrying. Then I said Look around, so you'll know who's got what, and where everything's at. My right saddle bag's got the first aid kit, flashlight and spare toilet paper, and the left one's got the horseshoe tools, stitcher and stuff. It'll get smoother, I promise you. With that we were off.

At first there were motorbikes and ATVs chasin' each other down the road to bother the horses, but by mid-morning we were off on a trail to ourselves, soon climbing a steep stretch that I thought might go better if we just got down and went a ways on foot to gave the horses a breather. At a notch in the hills we stopped and tied the horses, to have a look off to the south, where we could see the Rio Grande, and beyond it old Mexico, with some green that the map said was their national park. Off to the southeast we could also see our own Big Bend National Park. I told about the old Comanche Trail that ran up from the Big Bend all the way past Lubbock up into Oklahoma and Colorado and Kansas, where the Comanche would hunt in the summers before the first big cattle drives. I dug out a bag of carrots, gave one to each of the Mosleys and one to each of the horses just to keep everyone happy. Then we saddled up and picked our way down the pass and across the valley floor. A couple hours later we were climbing again, and near the top found a good patch of shade to step down and have lunch. It was just peanutbutter and jelly sandwiches and apples, but that meant the horses got another treat and the Mosleys kept makin' new friends.

By late afternoon we pulled into our second campsite, got un-packed and set up well before dark. The horses were quiet and tired from the day's workout, but glad to see we hadn't forgot 'em when we tossed out some hay, put a couple handfuls of grain in each feedbag, and topped up their water. I dug out a bunch of ribs that were half thawed, with barbecue sauce and some potatoes we scrubbed then stabbed a few times, smeared with butter and salted, wrapped in tin foil to tuck in around the fire. After they'd baked awhile, we set the grill on the coals and started to slather sauce on the ribs. I had a hunch we would have no trouble selling dinner to this crowd, who were watching the doings with interest.

Twenty minutes later I took my big fork to dish it up and said Grab you a plate and fork and come get it. The boys pushed their mama to the front, and had Eva laughing at their display of manners, swooping and bowing as they doffed their big hats. Soon we were all settled down with a plateful, and I'd passed around a canteen.

We ate everything, sucked every bone and licked our fingers, while the water boiled for coffee and cocoa. That night we didn't use lanterns at all. One of the things this park was known for was how dark it got, how grand the planets and stars and Milky Way paraded across the night sky. The campsites had no lights and no outlets, and we leaned back and just talked while we watched the constellations wheel overhead. I asked if any of them had been scared of the dark when they were little, and no one said a thing till Clint spoke up. He said his parents had moved from Minnesota when he was four, and the first night in the new place he'd been scared because of how strange Texas was, with all manner of wild things outside howlin' and yippin' their hearts out. The next day his dad had given him a brand-new flashlight with a button that clicked it on and off, and told him if he felt anything was scary, he should point the flashlight at it, and turn it on. When it went away he could turn it off again.

Mo said And did that work? Clint said You bet. And that's what we did with you boys.

The last thing we talked about that night wasn't stars but sleeping horses. They all knew that horses mostly slept standing. But then I talked about how the herd in the wild always had a dependable leader watching so a few horses at a time could lay down on the ground and sleep.

That's when they slept deeply, something they needed to do once in a while. But it showed the need for trust was deeply wired in them, as deep as the need to be able to run from attack. And I said I've been watching and hoping but none have laid down to sleep yet, not since we brought the two new brown ones into the herd. For over a year now Beulah had been watching while Lady and Lucky slept. I'd seen them do it a few times. But only recently would she sleep while Lucky watched. I don't know what's going to happen now, with two younger, stronger horses in the herd. It's about trust overcoming fear. I used to think that cowboys on roundup might get their horses to lie down and rest, if they were trusted enough. On this trip we might just find out.

The next morning Ike was up again early, while I was feeding the horses. I said Good morning, and asked how he was doing. He said I feel happy and a little sad. I said What do you mean? He said When I was laying there a while ago I thought how every bag on the horses would be lighter today because of what we ate an' did yesterday, and that they'll just keep getting lighter so the horses would be happier 'cause they'd have less to carry. But then for us every day would be one more gone we won't get back, one less we'll have till we need to go home.

I was leaning into the corral, watching the horses nosing and lifting the hay, tugging and chewing, not watching him. I said That's a pretty large thought, Ike. It's an old curse for humans, standin' both inside and outside their lives, feeling both. The thing about a trip like this is how every day we can get deeper in, get closer to what's here, an' closer to our real selves that have come all this way as mostly strangers. The one thing we might feel bad about is wasting what chances we get, what the old cowhands used to call burnin' daylight.

Ike said I think I see what you're sayin'. It's just hard to put a thing out of your head once it's in there.

Sure is. And hard not to get out ahead of yourself with your thinkin'. So do what I do.

What's that?

Let go and change the subject.

Okay. I was gonna ask you anyhow. Did any of the horses lie down to sleep last night?

Yes.

Aren't you gonna say which ones?

'Course, I only got a peek. But it was Beulah and Lady down sleepin'. And the three boys standing guard.

I'd never seen that boy grin so hard. He said That's a good sign, ain't it?

Yes. A sign we got a herd for sure.

Then we stirred up the fire, got going on bacon and eggs and toast for breakfast, with a couple of last night's baked potatoes chopped up in a pan. Some of the bread got a little black on one side, but we ate it all, then washed and packed, saddled and mounted up. It was a lovely early morning, with prairie birds singing by the hundreds, and the low sun suddenly blinding as it cleared the far rim. Today we had a wide sparse valley to cross, heading northwest. As we got to the far side and rose up into the hills there was more vegetation, with little trails weaving between the sagebrush and clumps of bitterbrush. I asked if anybody had a guess what made the trails.

Clint said Maybe deer. I said A good thought, and what I'd think if I hadn't read the history of this park, that used to be all one great big ranch. But that's a sure sign of sheep and goats, though there haven't been any here in maybe sixty years. In all those little eyes between the trails the plants were all eaten down to the roots, and are stunted. Cattle and horses won't chew it that close, 'less they're starvin'.

In the hills we came across a couple picnic tables with roofs for shade, and stopped to rest the horses while I passed some apples around. The horses got a few bruised ones, but didn't seem to mind. Ike said he'd heard a joke at school, What's worse than finding a worm in an apple? But Mo must have heard it and spoke up right away: Finding half a worm! We all roared, that made Eva turn her apple around and give it the eye. Ike said How did you catch the horses laying down last night? Didn't you sleep yourself? I said Old guys have to get up and pee in the night more than young fellas. So I got a couple chances to take a look around. And the corral's right there with all the horses together out under the starlight. So how's Beulah doing today? You notice any difference? Ike said She seems stronger and more wide-awake. But she's an awful good horse to begin with.

With that we mounted up and rode on. Occasionally we'd pass groups of hikers, some with dogs that would start barking at the horses. Supposed to be on a leash but mostly not. Still, our herd were mannerly and quiet, an' didn't take it wrong. We hadn't seen any other horses so far, but the season was early, and we were cheered to have the park mostly to ourselves. Every high point became a treat, a chance for the long view in all directions, to savor the emptiness, see the hawks hang and glide in the clear desert air. Every now and then we'd see a far-off building or two, that must be remnants of the ranch and its mining operations where hot work used to pay.

Then late in the day we rode up to our third campsite. We lifted the loads off the horses, then their saddles and bridles. This time the two brown horses started to roll in the corral and kick their feet in the air, and the rest soon joined them. Mo said What are they doing? Eva said Backscratching--feels good when you've been carrying all that stuff. Here, let me show you. She arranged us in a circle, and had us all scratching each others' backs till we were laughing and the boys were whinnying like little horses themselves.

Then I got the fire going, and a pressure cooker full of beans with diced onions and a ham hock on the boil, and a bunch of steaks soaking in teriyaki sauce. I wrapped more potatoes and carrots in tin foil with butter and salt, and tucked them in as the fire died down to coals. Then I asked everybody how they liked their steak, and grilled them that way while there was still light to see. Then we ate it all in such a hurry, that we could still see the grins on each others' faces in the twilight. Somebody said the meals just kept getting better, and I said that was the hunger talking.

The moon had been getting bigger since that first faint sliver the night we left home, and tonight the light on the plain below was strong and magical, everything casting a shadow. Off in the distance we could hear two coyote dens with their pups yapping and howling back and forth. We could also hear some kind of small burrowing owls calling too. I asked the boys what they thought they were saying, and Ike said You're not alone, we're out here too. Mo said The coyotes sound like they're havin' a party, then all of a sudden sound lonesome, like they're missin' somebody. I said Why don't you howl at 'em a little, and see if they'll talk back? So the boys tried conversing in yips and barks, but the coyotes shut right up. I asked Mo What's the matter? He said Somebody musta told 'em we wasn't coyotes.

A little later Ike asked, Do you think there are wild horses out here? I said On west of here there used to be, in New Mexico, and still might be mustangs in the mountains. But I haven't heard or seen sign of 'em so far. If there were any near, our horses would smell and hear them, and might get nervous. Ike said Why? I said On account of they're proof there's still a way to live without people. We all turned to look at the corral. The horses were standing quiet in the moonlight, still as statues.

I asked Clint and Eva if they did any camping when they were growing up. Clint said I got sent to a Christian summer camp, but the Christian part seemed to have nothing to do with nature or the outdoors, which was a shame. It was like two camps, one where we played and one where we prayed. We got to ride horses on some trails they had, but it was only once a week for a couple hours, twenty kids on twenty horses all in a line playing follow the leader. So it was like a lot of things there, canoeing and rowing, swimming and diving and archery, that we only got a taste of, then went back to the chapel, where we spent a lot of time thanking God for the meals and the beautiful world and practically everything except snakes and bats and mosquitoes. When I grew up I wasn't surprised to learn that at least snakes and bats had a real place in nature, what the minister called the grand scheme of things. But I've thought mosquitoes oughta fit in too, just haven't yet learned how they do.

Eva said after her dad died she lived in a suburb where about the only thing people did outdoors was mow their yards and wash their cars. She had a friend Brenda in sixth grade whose parents pitched a tent for the girls in the back yard, and she went over and they slept in sleeping bags and made S'mores on the barbecue grill and giggled half the night whispering about boys. Then she said But your ranch is realer and wilder than anything I ever saw.

I could see it was getting time for bed, but they didn't want to leave it here. So I pointed up at the sky and showed 'em how to find the Big Dipper and Polaris the North Star and a couple planets, Venus and Mars. When those coyote pups started up again, yipping and yapping, we all settled back in our bags and drifted off.

Then it was the morning of our fourth day. In the moonlight I'd seen our two brown horses lie down and sleep deep while the others watched over them. Things could hardly get any better for our little herd, with no squabbles or struggles at all. I was feeding the horses the mix in their feed bags, since we were out of hay till we got back to the trailer. But they seemed cheered and rested, and I got the boys to give 'em each a carrot while I got breakfast started.

Once the fire was going and the coffeepot on, I cut the bacon up into small pieces, and fried it with a couple cups of diced onion. Then I broke all the eggs we had left into our big pan, and stirred in the bacon and onion, while Clint was grating cheese that we heaped over it after I'd stirred in the salt and pepper. Then I dug a jar of salsa out and divvied up the scrambled eggs, with a piece of buttered toast apiece. And we ate like we'd been starved for days.

All our loads were getting smaller, and we had more room in the saddle. The horses were stepping more lively too. But we had to fill all the canteens and the water jug we had today, because tonight's camp would have no water. Today we would swing around on a trail to the northeast, then climb and dip through some of the roughest parts of the old ranch. Luckily one deep canyon followed a stream where we could water the horses along the way.

In the early hours we saw more wildlife than we'd seen so far. A golden eagle was hunting jackrabbits, circling on high, then tucking her wings to drop like a lightning bolt. Only minutes later we met a sidewinder, a small desert rattlesnake in the trail, that the horses needed no encouragement to steer clear of. And an hour later in the shade as we plunged into a narrow canyon, we came across a small herd of mule deer, feeding on the lush green along the quick clear water. Once the deer scampered off, we stopped in the shade to let the horses drink their fill from the stream and have a green bite. For the first time on the trip this day there were roadrunners darting along, seeming to race us. I never saw them eat a thing, though occasionally we'd spot things they were known to favor, like scorpions and beetles. But we remained in high spirits, cheered and at ease with it all.

When we stopped for lunch, we watered the horses again. For a silly change we made corned beef and Swiss cheese sandwiches, with apples all around. Then we climbed out of that canyon, and kept climbing on switchbacks until we got to the highest point on the old ranch. To the south we could see the Rio Grande and old Mexico again. I asked the boys what they thought of seeing another country, and Ike said it all looked like one country from up here, like at night when we looked at the Milky Way. To the north we could see low mountain ranges, and more high ground. While we had the horses tied in a line, I got my tools and checked their shoes, and found a couple nails that needed clinching again. Then we mounted up and rode gingerly down the other side, which was steeper in spots than I'd expected. But we all stayed in the saddle and didn't lose a thing.

As the trail eased down onto the desert floor it swung east, where there were patches of wild grasses, and more wild flowers than we'd seen so far. I was tempted to let the horses graze a little here, but we knew the rules: to carry all our own food and fuel, pack out our garbage, and not touch a thing in the park, dead or alive. We'd be fine without bothering anything.

Our fourth campsite came into view with an hour of daylight left. It had a corral too, but no water tap though a welcome surprise. The stock tank there still had a foot of rain water and snow melt in the bottom, that the horses found right away, before we could get their gear off. Then as they came up for air, Clint and I took down their bags and saddles, unlatched their bridles and set them free. The two brown horses again led the rest in rolling and kicking and stretching, that looked to become a regular thing.

I went off to start the fire and tackle dinner. I planned on chili and grilled cheese sandwiches, and got the pressure cooker on the grate with a mix of beans and spices to boil, then got a couple pounds of hamburger frying with chopped onions in the big skillet. While those things simmered I went back to the corral, to dish up some horse grain into their nose bags. I usually fed them in their pecking order, first Beulah, then Lady, then the two chocolate horses, then Lucky. But this time I reversed the order, feeding Lucky first, then Cicero and Nokey, then Lady and Beulah. Would they argue or squabble? Not a bit. It was like the old saying, I had 'em eating out of my hand. Maybe it was just the softening of old age, pushing and pulling at me, but their quiet patience had become a touching thing to see. Maybe every time a horse does what you want the deed's been earned, but it still feels at times like a gift.

I went back to the pots and added salt and pepper, chili spices, and a little of the cooking wine, a zinfandel in a box that might taste fine for grownups, even in our tin cups. Then I looked around, and realized all four of the Mosleys were sprawled out on their bags, sound asleep under the stunted trees. This day had been the hardest, climbing up and down and watching every step, yet we had covered close to 40 miles.

I let the beans cook another half an hour, then stirred in the meat and onions, and sliced up the cheese for grilled sandwiches. Dug out the bread and butter, laid the sandwiches out and put them together, then cleaned the big skillet and put it back on the grate. There wasn't much daylight left, just a pale sky and a purple haze off to the west, so I started waking them up with a quiet hint or two, as I set those buttered sandwiches sizzling in the pan. Right away they started to come around, Eva first, then Ike, then Clint, then Mo. Nobody wanted to miss anything, least of all dinner. There was a pile of bowls and plates, and a pile of spoons. And three tin cups full of wine.

This night was the full moon, and we all seemed to know it. They must have needed that nap, but it didn't dampen their appetites. I set the salsa out for the grownups, ladled the bowls of chili, cut the grilled cheese sandwiches and set them on plates. What more did we need? I had a canteen of cold water on hand, and the coffeepot on the grill full of water, in case the boys should want cocoa.

They ate the chili, went back to the pot and got more, went back till there was none left. Their quiet smiles were beautiful. The sandwiches got dipped in the chili, and also disappeared. Then I pulled a little box of cupcakes out of my saddlebag to pass around. We hadn't lit a lantern yet, and that night never would.

In the pale lavender light of false dawn I was up scouting the camp. The horses nickered their greetings, and I laid out their feed bags and filled them outside the corral. Then I went back to the order of oldest to youngest, that they seemed fine with. This would be our last day on the trail, back to that first camp we'd found in the dark, near the trucks and trailer in the lot nearby. This would be the hardest day for me not to plan, just let come and go its own way, no waving hellos or goodbyes. But as I leaned on the rail and watched the horses eat, I wondered what more I could want. You can't have it all, but this seemed like more than most ever got.

Then there was someone right next to me, and someone on the other side. It was Eva and Mo. They both reached out and touched me on either arm.

Hey Mr. Brick, did you sleep good?

Fine as frog hair, Mo. He giggled, then Eva asked after the horses, if I saw any down.

The only ones I saw down sleeping were the two youngest, Lucky and Cicero. She said, Looks like they must be done fighting.

You got that right. So let's get these feed bags off and go make some pancakes.

When the fire was going I fried up the last of the bacon, dug out butter and syrup, got the big skillet hot and started making flapjacks. The sizzle woke the others, and pretty soon we were all at it, lining our stomachs for the day. Then we rolled up our bags and saddled the horses.

As the sun rose there looked to be high dark clouds coming our way out of the west, but there was nothing to be done, and we were heading east on the last leg anyhow, so packed and loaded our gear to take off. I asked everyone to untie their rain slicker and keep it handy on the pommel, and a couple hours later a cloudburst caught us climbing up the far side of that first pass we'd crossed five days before. With a storm settled into the valley at the moment we couldn't even see the Rio Grande below. It got slippery, so we got down and put our slickers on, and tied the horses while the thunder rumbled in the mountains all around. But half an hour later the storm settled into a light rain that made the plain below smell fresh and alive. We climbed aboard, and slowly worked our way down. When we got to the foothills below the pass out ahead a busy little herd of javelinas crossed our track, the seven or eight of 'em an extended family snuffling along, weaving and darting, running hard. None of the Mosleys had ever seen one in the wild, and we reined up. The boys kept still in spite of themselves. Then just as we were set to move on, a cougar sprang out of the bushes, right under our noses, chasing those little wild pigs. The horses were already wound up, hadn't smelled or heard the cougar on account of the rain, so got startled.

They reared and wheeled. It was a close thing, felt like the horses might panic, somebody might get thrown. But the boys and their parents held on, kept their seats, and the horses didn't bolt. Like old cowhands would say, it was a whole lotta nothin', compared to what mighta been.

I stepped down and dug out some apples to give the horses. Eating those apples might help settle us one and all. Then as the rain lightened up, all at once the desert got positively noisy with bird chatter. We hardly saw a bird, but mighta waited all year for this moment and still missed hearing the desert spring to life all around, with songs that rattled on and on like sweetly scissored applause.

We'd missed lunch for the first and only time, but thought we should just keep going. Then it wasn't long before the trail eased back down to the road, and we loped the last half-dozen miles single-file, clopping along on the shoulder. Seemingly all on their own the horses lined themselves up from oldest to youngest, with Ike on Beulah riding lead, and me on Lucky riding drag. As the rain slowed to nothing, the road steamed in the bright sun. The gang all knew where they were going, and turned into the right corral. Once we got the saddles off, we filled the water tank while the horses rolled and waggled their hooves in the air, got good and muddy until they all looked alike. We walked over to the trailer in the parking lot to get the horses more hay, and find a brush and currycomb, then built a fire, and sorted through the food bags to see what we had left. I dug down to the bottom, and sure enough, there was still a half-frozen block of pork chops wrapped up, ready and waiting. So it would be fried pork chops, potatoes, peppers and onions. Everybody helped wash and slice the potatoes, peppers and onions, while I thawed and breaded the pork chops. Clint filled the big skillet with the veggies and kept stirring it, while I laid the chops out on the grill. Then half an hour later the only sound in camp was the melody of tin-plate eating as the sun slid down a blazing western sky.

We tossed more wood on the fire, and packed away everything but the coffeepot and coffee and cocoa, then settled back. I asked if anybody thought we should pitch the tent. I stood facing west and south, looking for clouds, but by now it was clear to the horizon. I thought it wouldn't be a bad idea to put the tent up for practice anyhow, since we'd had the luck of great weather all week, and practice is how you make luck--so we did, but then lay back down around the fire.

I said What did you think of today? Mo said This is the wild west for sure. We talked about the animals we saw. Eva had never seen a golden eagle, or javelina, or cougar in the wild. Or even a rattlesnake. I said I had a question for them. Did anybody bring a camera? And if you didn't, why not? Ike said We talked about that at home, and since we'd never seen you take a picture, and didn't see hardly a one in your house, we figured maybe cowboys didn't need to take pictures. Now we all have a picture in our heads of an eagle hunting jackrabbits, and a cougar hunting wild pigs, that won't get lost or faded, that'll be with us always.

Then Clint said Mr. Brick, what's the picture in your head from this trip, that won't go away? And I said How those horses come together, and joined us. When they didn't freak out about the javelinas we weren't just lucky, then when that cougar showed. They were all set to do what we wanted. And since we didn't freak out, neither did they. And for that I say thanks all around.

Next morning I rolled out early, lit a fire in the pale light for coffee, then fed the horses hay and what feed was left, in their nose bags. I figured only Clint and I might need coffee, so when they woke I told everyone I would buy us breakfast in Alpine, in an hour or so, at a little place I knew that cooked some great French Toast. Meanwhile we had hot drinks, and if someone would help me pack up the tent and load horses, we'd soon be set to roll.

Prairie Dog Heaven

That trip south gave us things to think and talk about for weeks. And the horses wore a glow and attitude that didn't quickly fade. Out in the big pasture they stuck together, played and moved around like a herd. And they seemed eager for us all to go for a ride. The boys wore their big hats and boots back to school Monday, and in the telling recalled details they'd prit'near forgot. Sitting around the fire pit past Monday supper, I said I'd forgot to mention a few things myself. Like what, Eva said. I said Like the night before last that was a full moon, the horses all turned their tails to the moon and hid their heads, like it was too bright and might keep 'em awake otherwise. And who knows, maybe it did. The couple times I peeked, they were all up on their feet that night, but for the two youngest geldings down sleeping, Lucky and Cicero.

I asked the boys what came out in the telling at school. Mo said when that cougar jumped out of the bushes, he remembered petting Lady's neck. She was all set to jump anyhow, felt like she was made outa springs. Ike said I thought Beulah wasn't scared like the others, she stood so still in the middle with her head up. But then I saw her eyes were big as saucers and knew I had to calm her down, talk to her. I knew if I hadn't been on her she'da run away for sure.

I asked what the kids at school thought. Mo said a couple of 'em wondered if we had a gun. But I told 'em What for? We're not supposed to shoot anything in the park. Clint said, That's a good thought, son. Besides, there was too many of us. That cougar wasn't going to bother five big people on five big horses, he was after those tasty little pigs. Though I bet he was hungry, I said. Cougars and javelinas both mostly hunt at night. Clint said It was pretty dark there with the rain beatin' down, that likely covered any sound of the cat's approach. He mighta thought he stood a good chance to get fed.

Ike said somebody in his class wanted to know if we wore helmets, like he'd seen cowboys wear to ride bulls. Eva said What did you tell him? Ike said We have good horses, not motorcycles, so we get to wear hats that keep the sun and rain off our heads.

Then I told them one other thing I'd forgotten to say over breakfast in Alpine. My great aunt Mayella and her family had built a cabin around Alpine that I heard about when I was small but never saw. Her husband was a railroad man, ran a station east of Dallas, so they got a free ride across the state every summer with their kids. In Alpine they rented horses and went camping in the mountains and empty back country. One thing Mayella always talked about was how hard the windstorms blew in Alpine. She said they had a rug in their cabin that sometimes hovered half a foot off the floor made of boards with half-inch gaps in-between. They'd built the cabin up on stone blocks with its floorboards spaced apart to be cool in summer, but when they spent one Christmas there they were surprised how cold it was. She said They'd had to crack the ice in the water bucket to make tea, and finally plugged all those gaps to keep out the snakes and scorpions.

We planned a little picnic ride on the open range for the second Saturday of April, at that state grazing land where I'd taken the boys once before, a few years back. Now that we had enough good horses there would be no stopping us. I said we could even plan to ride a little ways after dark, if they didn't mind. And the Mosleys were all for it. When Eva asked the boys what they'd like to eat, Mo said Cowboy food.

So the night before, we cooked up and packed a cold dinner of fried chicken, potato salad and pie, with a lunch of meatloaf and pickle sandwiches, with granola bars, apples and carrots for snacks. And stuffed the two nylon bags in the fridge. Before dawn that morning I fed the horses, and while they ate I hitched the fifth wheel trailer to the truck, cleared all the tools and stuff out of the back seat that like to gather there so we'd have room. It was a little under two hours each way, but we'd all manage to fit in. Clint showed up to help me buckle the halters on the horses and load them in. They could tell something was up, and were steaming in the cool air, watchful and quiet, with no complaints.

I've always liked being underway before the first real slice of sunlight, though I'm still not sure why. Maybe I don't think I'm gonna get what I want, and just wanta be sure and see whatever's comin' my way anyhow. I do know when I'm done sleepin' I might as well be up, and once I got my boots and hat on I'm about set to roll.

With the trailer full of horses it comes alive, shaking around with all of them finding their footing, getting set for the ride. I know horses don't much care for trailers, so I try to be in no hurry, ease into turns and stops and keep it smooth so they don't get tossed around.

When the horses had got settled, we were off. The truck stayed quiet till we got to the open range land and pulled off at a wide shoulder about nine in the morning, let down the tailgate and unloaded the horses. Then we tossed up the saddles, tightened the girths and put on the bridles, and mounted up for the ride.

Coming back here I remembered how two years ago Mo used to skip to keep up with Ike, but now they fell in step like their horses did. And they took polite turns telling their parents every little thing I'd said about the place, without me opening my mouth. How way off to the south the land followed the curve of the earth. How far it was to the edge. Maybe someday soon I'd have it all said and could just lope along as quiet as my horse.

There had been a few changes. Today there were some cattle nearby, and we'd probably get a close look, but wouldn't want to bother them. We had more horses and more people, that were all used to each other, traveling together. We'd been here in the fall, but this was spring. I could hear whippoorwill and mourning doves, and sometimes in the distance thought I heard red-winged blackbirds, that made me think of water. We had canteens, but really not enough water for the horses, so I figured we'd have lunch once we found some. So I said Why don't we head for the largest bunch of cattle, who won't be far from water, if they're not standin' in it, and might have a clue where to look. We just want to ease up on them, not bother or spook 'em, and see if we can figure out where they're wettin' their whistles.

By the time we reached the cattle and their calves I could hear those red-winged blackbirds again for sure, a little off to the west. So we swung wide and soon found a stretch of marsh, with cattails and red-winged blackbirds and a few wild ducks. It was fed by a creek probably filled by spring and winter storms, that went dry in summer, but it was here now, and the horses waded in and nosed until they drank their fill.

We rode on a mile or two past the cattle, and found some lush grass on a little hillside to have lunch. I strung my lariat between a couple big strong sagebrushes, and hitched the horses along the line with halters and leads. Then we tossed off their saddles and unpacked the sandwiches and snacks. It was a fine spring day, and we could see an occasional hawk riding the thermals, on the lookout for prey.

Eva said When we got out of the truck I thought this was all flat empty grass. But it turns out to be rough and wild, full of all kinds of life. In summer I bet it gets to look more like desert than prairie. I said Depends on the weather, and how many animals the ranchers graze. You're seeing it more lively and overgrown than it gets all the rest of the year. This is about when the cattle and horses like it best, right after the rains. This is when ranchers turn their cows and calves out to feed on the tender new growth.

While the grownups were lounging and eating, the boys had wandered off. Just then they came dashing back, running on their tiptoes. Clint said What is it, boys? Ike said A baby fox! It lives in a hole in the ground. So we all jumped up to go see. Over a little rise they pointed at a hole hidden beneath a big sagebrush. There was a little fox, mostly gray, who was picking up what looked like little red gloves one at a time, and putting them back in the burrow.

I called the boys over, and said we needed to give that fox lots of room. That's a kit fox, not a baby but a grownup mommy. A rare one. See how big her ears are? That's how she cools herself while she listens to you. Those things that look like red gloves are her babies, that have just barely opened their eyes. She's tryin' to hide 'em away and keep 'em safe.

Mo said Are they dangerous? No, I said, They're our friends. A gray fox would be three times her size, but these little ones mostly live in the desert. They eat scorpions, sidewinders and lizards, and whatever else they can catch--kangaroo mice, packrats and other small critters. She's probably here for the water and greenery, and her mate must be nearby, out on the hunt for their supper.

After lunch we fed the horses a few apples, then got saddled up and set to move. We'd just climbed on our horses when Ike pointed at a red-tailed hawk that swooped down at the kit fox den, but the sagebrush in the way let the kit fox dive down her hole just in time. Still, it was spring, and everything was astir with new life and a search for mates, both predators and prey.

As we headed south the horses spread out five abreast and fell in step, since there were few trails and no trees out here anyhow. The day felt as wide open as the land, with foothills to the east and mountains faint knotted, tabled and domed presences far off to the west. I asked Ike and Mo if they thought the horses remembered being here before. They both said You betcha. Clint said They must love the smells and sounds, with no distractions. I said This is the kind of land horses came from, where they thrived before humans ever got close to one.

We were chatting along drifting south till all at once the line of horses of their own accord wheeled to the west. Straight ahead was a patch of prairie a quarter mile across, that looked like it had been mowed, that had a sentinel, maybe eighteen inches tall, posted every few yards. And they were all barking back and forth, passing around a sharp warning--about us. It was a prairie dog town.

This one was nothing to some I had seen, that could be several square miles. This was no more than a village really, but it was bustling, though all we could see were some burrows and sentinels and short grass. And on the far side, in a ways from the manicured edge where the burrows and sentries ended were a cow and her calf grazing peacefully. They paid the prairie dog chatter no mind.

We all pulled up a couple hundred feet short to keep our distance and take in the scene. Though these rodents seemed at times to be barking at us, when we looked at the offenders, they turned slightly away, as if addressing someone else. But this in truth seemed like one of Coronado's seven lost cities of gold, bright in the afternoon sun, with all the inhabitants identically cloaked like tiny monks. They might as well have been in disguise because they all looked alike to the casual eye. They could be males or females, sons or daughters, grandparents or grand-babies. They could be town officials, or gossips and busybodies, town criers or well-trained sentries on duty. One of these rodents could well believe he was master of all he surveyed.

We sat quiet, and the horses stood easy and motionless, so eventually the sentries quieted, and were joined by others up from underground to squat and watch the show. Eva said What are you thinkin', Brick? I said Henry David Thoreau wrote in Walden that every house is but a porch at the mouth of a burrow. I think this is about what he meant.

That big red-tailed hawk musta been tagging along after us, because just then her shadow swooped low over the town, and the swath of prairie dogs right in her path tumbled down their holes. It was like bowling with an invisible ball. The cow and her calf didn't bother looking up, though as soon as the hawk passed, the sentinels popped right back up, full of indignant chatter.

The boys were full of questions as we sat and watched, and I tried to answer without stirring up prairie dog outrage. Ike asked Are all the burrows hooked together? I said Some neighbors are, although each burrow is mostly one family, or extended family. There are little rooms for sleeping and nurseries and storage. And there is always a back door, an escape hatch. You see those cones built up around most of the burrows? They're so the sentries sit up higher and see farther. And also to manage the runoff, so big storms don't flood 'em out of their holes.

While we chatted a little, Mo was uncommonly silent. Finally I asked what he was thinking.

I just want to get down and play with them. But I'm a little scared. I want to throw them something and see what they do.

Like what?

A ball, or pine cone maybe.

What do you think they might do?

I don't know. Play catch. I don't really know what they'd do.

They're wild animals, Mo.

I know.

Then what do you really want? He thought about it hard for a minute.

I'd like 'em to do what they do when there's nobody watching 'em. What they do when they don't have to be on the lookout.

I think I know what you mean. But they're little wild things, and lots of other things eat 'em. So they have to act like there's always somebody watching 'em. This is the only way they have of protecting themselves, by warning each other, so they can all run and hide. So they're always barking. If they had words, what do you think they'd be saying?

Watch out, there, watch out.

Then he said, Can we give them something?

I dug out a couple of carrots, and the boys urged their horses closer, then broke pieces off and threw them around to different sentries standing there. At first the prairie dogs sounded the alarm, but their cries changed, and soon they all seemed to want a taste of what the boys were offering. Then we touched up the horses and rode around the village and on to the south.

When that prairie dog town was out of sight I suddenly remembered the biggest one I'd ever heard about, and dropped back to tell Clint and Eva about it. Vernon Bailey, a wildlife biologist who did surveys of a bunch of western states, in 1905 described a vast prairie dog metropolis that stretched 250 miles north from San Angelo to Clarendon, that was about a hundred miles wide, and covered some 25,000 square miles of West Texas. He estimated that it was home to 400 million black-tailed prairie dogs just like these. I'd also read that today prairie dog habitat was only one percent of what it had been then. Clint and Eva looked at me and shook their heads, and we rode on quiet a while.

The day was getting along, and we needed to think about supper. A couple miles south of the prairie dog town we found a little rise with some sagebrush nearby. I strung out my lasso between two strong bushes again, took off the horses' bridles, put on their halters and leads, tied them to the picket line and tossed their saddles down. Then we spread a couple blankets and opened the duffle bag of cold chicken, potato salad and pie. While we ate Mo was still stirred up, thinking of prairie dogs, and asked what they ate. I said mostly greens and seeds, with some bugs and grubs. He said they sure seemed to like those pieces of carrot. I said I bet they never had any carrot before. He wondered if they'd make good pets. I looked at Clint and Eva, but they shrugged and let me answer. I said they live in families and neighborhoods and towns, so just one might get pretty lonesome. Then I told about some farm kids I'd known in grade school, who found a baby raccoon in the woods that had lost its mama and brought it home. At first it was like any baby, just wanted to sleep and drink milk, cuddle and poop a little, but after a month or so it wasn't a baby any more. That raccoon could climb the drapes and the roof and all over, could get into anything, chewed the pillows and furniture for fun, till their parents said they had to get rid of it. They called the state fish and game office, and were told they couldn't keep a wild animal anyhow. So they took it several miles away to a state wildlife refuge, but the raccoon found its way back the next day. So finally they took it in a boat across a big river, and dropped it in the woods over on the other side. It didn't come back after that, but those kids always wondered how it did, if it made it okay in the wild.

Then I said how about if you boys give the horses an apple, then we'll all have a piece of pie. By the time we were done the sun was low in the west, and we would need to start back, so we saddled and bridled the horses. While everyone was climbing up and getting settled, I rode a loop around our picnic spot, and spotted something we'd missed. Just a bit to the south was a little pond maybe fifteen feet across. I pulled up and soon everyone else was gathered around. I mentioned that the horses didn't want to drink there, that the water smelled rank from where we sat, and the horses stood aloof, as if understanding all that I said.

In summer it'd be dry and overgrown, all but invisible. But the horses would still know what it was.

The boys said What is it?

A buffalo wallow, an ancient one that still holds water in spring. Probably haven't been buffalo hereabouts since the 1870s, nigh on 150 years. They'd use it in spring, to wallow and roll around to get rid of their shaggy winter coat--which gives it that smell, and why horses won't drink here. In the summer the buffalo would roll in the dust to get rid of biting flies.

And without another word we headed north. With the sunset in all its glory, a steady wind out of the south picked up as we were passing the prairie dog town on the other side. A few prairie dogs were barking out their warnings as we rode past, though it was surprising how quick they quieted. Ike called out What do you think, Mr. Brick? They must feel like they know us.

I saw the mama cow and her calf still there, and noticed mama had a limp and pointed it out to Ike, who held back his horse to let me catch up.

Mr. Brick, why is that cow still here?

I think she feels safer with all these lookouts around. Barkin' to warn her of trouble.

I told Ike how government ag agents used to say that prairie dogs were a danger to horses and cattle, that livestock could step in their holes and break their legs--but that rarely happens. They were lookin' for an excuse to poison the prairie dogs, and get rid of everything that fed on them, from eagles to cougars to coyotes and the little gray prairie wolves there used to be. The buffalo never stepped in their holes and broke their legs either. In fact, buffalo and pronghorn antelope and finally cattle liked to graze the short grass kept mown by prairie dogs around their towns, since the sentries would bark an alert when there was danger around.

With the sun below the horizon, the prairie grass flared red and gold against the sky as the wind groomed and ruffled its surface, while the day faded and died. And in single file we moved on. Under a pale lavender sky the prairie seemed expectant, as if waiting for something. A lone bird might fly over, then a late string of birds heading somewhere together to rest. I hoped the boys recalled how magical it had been their first time, two years back.

We all noticed how Beulah moved to take the lead and the other horses fell in line as the dark arrived. I hung back to be sure no one felt left out, and brought up the rear. The south wind was still blowing for a while after dark, that might make our back trail to the truck a little harder to find by nose. But soon the afterglow faded, and stars appeared, then the distant Milky Way, solemn and deep, faintly scattered across the night sky. The music of our gear creaking and jingling joined with the spring sounds of cicadas, crickets, peepers and owls, that grew louder as we came upon that patch of swampy ground near where we'd had lunch. I asked if anybody could feel that little damp in the air, and said Let's see if the horses are thirsty. It only seemed like a couple minutes till Beulah's hooves splashed at the water's edge, and the other horses fanned out on either side and lowered their heads to lip the water.

Eva whispered That's amazing--I can't see a thing but the stars. That might as well be the whole show anyhow. Clint answered Feels like we're out on the edge of a giant merry-go-round, pretending to steal a ride.

Soon Beulah lifted her head, backed up and turned to the north. All the horses seemed to put their heads together a moment, then Beulah moved into the lead again, followed by Lady, then Nokey and Cicero, then Lucky. Over the next hour the moon rose and climbed the sky, half a moon that seemed plenty in this clear air, and the horses moved with a little more confidence. And I could see the riders grinning. Ahead we started to hear the cattle we had weaved through early in the day. They could hear us coming, and were lowing a little. They couldn't see us very well, and as we approached, every now and then a cow would scamper off a few steps, then stop to see if she was in the clear. I said Let's just keep it slow and quiet, so we don't bother 'em. This was the smiling dreamy part of the ride, a trance in the moonlight where we fell silent, as if reluctant to break the spell. The horses kept single-file, but their tails were twitching and sweeping, their ears up listening to the night sounds, their heads nodding in time with each step.

Then up ahead faint and pale the truck and gooseneck trailer stood, awash and bleached in moonlight. We stepped down and tied the horses to cleats along the side, and hugged and laughed with relief. I found the last of the apples and carrots, and put the animals' halters on, then the boys thanked them and fed them what we had. We turned the trailer lights on, led the horses in and tied them in order for the ride home.

     I pulled out and eased the trailer around. Then as we started north for home, Ike leaned forward from the back seat and said, You know what, Mr. Brick? I've missed being out with the horses, out on the open range. Thanks for takin' us back. I don't know that I'll ever get enough.

     On the long ride home the boys soon drifted off, but Clint and Eva wanted to talk, so they leaned close, and we kept it quiet. They wanted to know why I thought riding in the dark was good for us and the boys. I said It's worth a little effort to feel at home out here, at least unafraid and calm. I told them how I hadn't been to sea except for the troop transport ship from San Diego to Saigon and back, when I was in the Army, but being at sea at night felt a little like being out horseback on the dark prairie. At first you're overwhelmed, thinking of what could be out here, how all directions look the same, how much water there is under you--three miles and more. But there's not much to fear, a collision of waves that might splash up and catch you off-guard, maybe, an occasional bird cry or sound that could be a whale blowing as it breaks the surface. Once your eyes and ears have got used to the dark endless motion, something in you nods in time with it, just like the horses do. This world may feel dangerous, but it's mostly not, it's mostly indifferent to our passing as it goes through the aeons about its mindless business. These moments outside the manmade world remind us of our place in the scheme of things--as parts of something larger and stronger, more ancient and more knowing than ourselves.

Flop-eared Fly-Chaser

I was thinkin' it was time for a few more cowhand lessons for the boys, then got lucky in town at the little one-chair barber shop for my twice-a-year haircut, that lets my hat wobble on my head a week or so. The fella waitin' next to me in line was Scattergun Gleason, an old farmer who'd played minor league baseball in his youth, back when it seemed like more fun an' less tricky than these days. He'd been comin' in long as I had, and was a customer Bernie had enjoyed before he'd sold me his land and this new guy Ramon Devlon his shop. I'd long ago heard how Scattergun had got his name in his first official at-bat, knocked fourteen foul balls in a row all over then bounced a double off the right field wall. Today we happened to be talkin' about sad and sorry-looking folks whose whole lives looked like they'd been dealt a bad hand at cards. Some who forgot or plain never learned how to laugh or play, much less make someone else laugh. Then all at once he said Speakin' of sorry-lookin', you ever seen a baby mule? I said I'd seen young mules in harness aplenty, and an endless supply of old mules, even worked a few, but could never recollect as I'd seen a baby mule. For that matter, I hardly knew where they came from, except how you'd need a mare horse and a donkey jack to get set up in business.

I said In fact when I was a boy I heard most all the mules in the country came from a couple big Missouri breeding outfits. They ran a regular circuit around the South through cotton and tobacco country, herds of hundreds from Virginia through the Carolinas down to Florida and out to east Texas on the back roads early each spring sellin' mules. The circuit was mostly sale barns with regular auctions, that ran mules through pretty quick 'cause they were cheaper than horses, with less profit, and the buyers were all lookin' for cheap young muscle to work the hot sun, not much else. A few might be lookin' for saddle mules to pick their way through the back country, but in that case they'd mostly keep an eye peeled when the U.S. Army went to sell off some surplus. And not a soul was ever lookin' at mules to win a beauty contest.

When I'd said all I knew, Scattergun told me it so happened he had a baby mule just born on his place. I said Do you mind if I come out have a look? Scatter said Lookin's free, why the hell not? It might just be love at first sight. We shared a chuckle at that while Ramon the barber brushed a man off, spun him around for the reveal and got paid, then came my turn in the chair. Getting up I got Scatter's phone number and where to find his mailbox, and we were set.

I don't know what I expected, but knew I'd always liked mules. They were smart, and circumspect. Some cow hands had no use for 'em, thought they were stubborn, vindictive, and only for farmers, but the truth was they were part of a past not many cared to talk about, the world of slavery and then sharecropping all over the South. The promise after the Civil War of forty acres and a mule never materialized, but it should have, and said right where mules stood, one at a time working forty acres, share-cropped nigh-unto death.

That next Saturday I asked the boys if they cared to go for a ride. I told 'em I needed to look at some animals, but said no more, just that We oughta take the horses out when we get back. Scattergun lived this side of town, so it wasn't a long ride, and I'd called ahead first to make sure he was home and inclined toward visitors.

So I found his blue mailbox with Gleason lettered on it in white paint, with a Wiffle ball stuck up on a rusty piece of threaded rod instead of a little red flag. We pulled into his barnyard, parked out of the way in the weeds, and were just climbin' out when he stepped down off his porch. I introduced him to Ike and Mo as Scattergun Gleason, though I knew his front name to be Jeffrey. When folks have garnered a little fame, there's no harm letting new folks in on the show, that I thought the boys might enjoy. Here were two underage cow hands in their boots and hats, and here was a fella older than me, in overalls an' a long-sleeved blue work shirt turned up two turns at the wrist, with an engineer cap on his head. But farmer or no, he had played ball for serious, and got paid for the playin' ten years in a row. Which for these boys was a lifetime.

So while we were walkin' toward the barn I asked him how he got his name, and the boys got to hear the whole story. How he swung fifteen times in a row and never missed, just slapped at 'em and hit 'em all over.

Tell me, Scatter, were you just showin' off, or lookin' for a particular pitch, or what?

Well, Brick, it was my first trip to the plate, my first game in the league. You could say I was lookin' to make an impression. The skipper an' the battin' coach were none too happy when they give me the take sign an' I hit a foul home run down the first base line, then they give me another take sign an' I hit another foul home run down the third base line. After I fouled off four pitches they quit sendin' signs at all, since the fans were stirred up an' all raisin' a ruckus. This was a team an' a pitcher that I'd heard had been givin' us fits. And it was the second inning, nothin' to nothin', with our best runner on first. An' here was their big horse of a kid throwin' hard, an' he couldn't put a one past me. Fourteen pitches, fourteen foul balls, just wearin' him down. Then the skipper stepped out of the dugout and give me the old slash across his throat, so I hit one for serious, bounced off the right field wall for a double, that drove in a run. An' we went on to win that game. They pulled their best pitcher in the fourth inning, as I was comin' up to bat again.

Do you miss it sometimes, Scatter?

Only every day. Though I can't hit like I used to. And everybody knew the story from my nickname from the first, how I wouldn't take signals on my first at-bat, so nobody would ever put my name in the hat for a reg'lar coachin' job.

The boys just watched the two of us, back an' forth. Then we walked into the barn, an' a couple stalls back he had a big rangy bay mare with this funny-lookin' dark little creature in the straw next to it, quiet and calm as a baby bat. I asked Scatter how old she was, and he says Day before we got our hats lowered, so three days old. He says Here, let's take 'em out in the sunshine, so you get a decent look. With that, he snapped a lead onto the mare, and led her out of the stall. Right away the baby heaved up and trotted after mama. The little mule wasn't shaky or wobbly or nothing. For three days old she was goin' fine, side to side an' back and forth, practically dancin' end for end.

Scatter walked them out to a small pasture, and let us through the gate with him. Ike said Mr. Scatter, can we pet her? Scatter said We'll just have to see if Dolly lets you, since mama is boss. But if you're nice an' quiet she just might. Mo said I got a apple in my pocket. Scatter said That'll work for Dolly, but the mule just started nursin', an' wouldn't know what to do with hard food just yet. But we might try this. He reached in his pocket and pulled out a Wiffle ball. So Mo palmed the apple for Dolly, that seemed to suit her just fine. Then while she was busy with it, Scatter rolled the Wiffle ball out in front of the baby mule. The baby danced right out and rolled the ball back and forth with her nose. She tried to pick up the ball, but it wouldn't fit in her mouth, just a shade too big around.

Scatter said I'm thinkin' in a few weeks I might have her chasin' balls for battin' practice, soon as her mouth gets big enough to pick up the ball.

Mo said Does she have a name? Scatter said I ain't thought a one yet, but like a mule I'm all ears. Ike thought that was funny, but Mo was dubious. Scatter said What's the matter? Mo said You aint gonna call her Ears, are you? Scatter said Why not? Mo said She can't help it havin' big ears. It's not hardly fair. Scatter said You got a point there, Mo. So what does she remind you of?

Mo turned and looked at the baby mule playing with the ball. Makes me think a somethin' that can flutter around a little. Like a moth, or a flying squirrel. What do you think, Mr. Brick?

I said Scatter told me in the barber shop that she was sorry-looking. I have to disagree. That mule looks solemn even when she's playin'. Serious an' sober as a baby judge. Her legs are so long it's like she's got that tiny little body up on stilts. Puts me in mind of a baby giraffe. Scatter said And for a little while those legs just seem to get longer. Mules appear to take more time than a horse to catch up to themselves. I don't know what we oughta call her. I never named a mule before.

Ike said I like Stilts. Or Serious. Somethin' for how she looks at us. Scatter says What do you mean? She squints. Huh, Scatter says. Squints.

Scatter went over and picked up the ball she was nosing, and tossed it a ways. The little critter ran right after it, but then stopped before she got there, and turned back to her mama.

You see that? Talk about smarts. Only took the second throw to figure she can't pick it up, so why bother. Scatter was pleased as punch.

Turned out the boys went back with me a couple more times to visit that baby mule and see how she was gettin' on. Scattergun went to a pet store and bought her a red rubber ball that was a little smaller than the Wiffle ball, with a bell and a squeaker inside. When he'd toss her the ball she'd run after it, snatch it up and shake her head to ring the bell, then trot back to him chewing the thing so it would squeak like crazy. Then she'd drop it at his feet and nod up an' down, for him to throw it again.

Scatter started calling her Blinken, he said because of how she fell asleep a little at a time. She'd keep opening her eyes when he thought she'd dozed off. The boys liked her new name, and took it up right away. They also liked her new ball, and noticed that she knew the two different sounds it made, and chose which one to use.

The boys talked about Blinken so much that their folks got interested, and the next time we went they came along for the ride. Eva said she expected her to be like a little clown, and wasn't prepared for how sober and wise she could be. I said You know how comedians are, how the best ones don't laugh at their own jokes, just pantomime like Buster Keaton and Charlie Chaplin. Clint said But she's really playful, like a dog. Except she doesn't smile or let her tongue hang out.

Just then Scattergun pulled out a bat and hit a hot grounder with that red rubber ball. And Blinken was off like a shot, galloping after it. She'd snapped it up before it stopped rolling, cantered back while chewing and shaking it to get both sounds going, and dropped it at Scatter's feet. He slapped down another grounder and Blinken tore out after it. I asked him if he'd tried her on any pop flies, and he said he wasn't sure how good she could focus on a ball in the air, but said he'd give it a try. And while she watched he hit a pop fly. She ran after it, and had the line right, but when the ball came down it hit her on the rump, which she didn't like. Scatter

walked out and picked up the ball, shook and squeezed it till the little mule
took it out of his hand. She ran to Dolly with it in her mouth, shaking
and chewing it, but when her mama turned away she dropped the ball and
ducked her head to nurse a little.

Scatter said She does so good with this noisy ball in the grass, for
now I think I'll just stick with the grounders.

The last time the boys and I went back to see Blinken she was a little over a year old. She was still floppy and silly, and liked playing ball with
Scattergun. But it was mostly fetch. She had learned to wait for the ball to
hit the ground to chase it, but seemed to be at an awkward age, big enough
not to be shy, but not sure how to behave around people or Scatter's other
livestock. But she was still quiet, an' still had those ears like a baby bat. Scatter asked me what I'd be doing if I was raising a young horse. I told him I'd
put a halter on her and lead her around, get her to follow. Don't make 'em
long lessons, never get in a tug-o-war, and reward her by talking to her and
petting her, not just treats. Now is when you oughta decide what you want
her to be--a plow mule or a pack mule or a saddle mule. Or all three. She's
so smart all you gotta do is make her want what you want, and she might
take a minute to study it, but then should come right along.

On the ride home Ike asked if I liked how Blinken had changed.
Before I could say a thing, Mo said She can't help it. I said It's that way
with all young animals. First they're cute as a bug's ear, and everything they
think or do is full of wonder at the world that's brand-new all around. But
then they hit kind of a rough patch, maybe because their bodies get too
big too quick, and they trip over their feet and bang their heads into things
they didn't need to duck under just last week. Ike said It sounds like you're
talkin' about us. And I answered No offense. I could just as well be tellin' on
myself.

Then out of the blue Mo said, I got a different question I keep
forgettin' to ask. Why do you always park in the weeds over at Scattergun's
place? I said I guess 'cause the weeds tell me right where no one else parks,
especially those that live and work on the place. It's just to stay outa their
way, an' be polite.

Boys' Night Out

As the boys kept busy at their riding work and play around the horses and cattle, late that summer I started to think I'd been too hard on the matter of rodeos. After all, the word just meant "roundup" in Spanish, and most cowboys had the urge to show off their skills at handling livestock, since their best moves mostly happened with no one around to cheer, much less pick up the pieces. So I thought I'd bring up the idea of going to a local rodeo late in August. The Switzer County Rodeo was a local affair that didn't draw the big-name competitors, but had most of the usual events. So first I mentioned it to Clint and Eva around the Mosleys' firepit after the boys were in bed, and we talked it over. Neither of them had ever been to a rodeo, but after I laid out a few of the pros and cons, they thought the boys could make up their own minds. I asked if they'd care to come along, but they said they'd appreciate having a breather.

So when I mentioned it the next night to Ike and Mo, they were on me in a heartbeat. Sure they wanted to go, but Ike right off said he thought I didn't like rodeos. I said I'd always admired a good show, but there were a couple things that had kept me from doing it for fun or profit. Some animals were mistreated, or made mean by impatient cowboys wanting more than they had to give. And some events were plain dangerous, to where the prize might not even pay the winners' hospital bills. Besides, winning sometimes seemed as much a matter of luck as of talent, despite how some cowboys proclaimed they were just fulla "try" with no "quit." But I promised them we'd get to see some fine horses doing smart things, and smart cowhands doing fine things, and to top it off some ferocious bulls out to prove they weren't born to be ridden.

Clint and Eva just watched and grinned as we talked it over. Likely they thought I'd gotten my hands full this time. Finally I told them the rodeo was next weekend, and said how about if we go give it a try Saturday, when there'd be plenty of new things to see.

So that Saturday the boys knocked early and we made stacks of pancakes and sausages, poured on the syrup and gobbled 'em down, then washed the dishes and headed out by ten, to be there when the grounds opened at noon. There was to be a grand parade through town, out to the fairgrounds, but we skipped that. Instead we parked and found good seats in the shade in the stands, before they filled up. And there we sat eatin' roasted salt peanuts washed down with lemonade when the riders swirled into the big ring in two loops that galloped round the fence, then met and lined up in the middle. The outer ring was mostly performers and contestants, young boys and girls in bright new outfits, with white hats, fringes and sparkles, while the inner ring was celebrities--the mayor and county commissioner, sponsors and other luminaries. Right away on the outer ring Ike spotted that skinny girl we'd seen four or five years back at O'Grady's Auction barn, when we'd bought Lucky. She was older, taller, and shapelier, with long pale shining hair that matched the mane and tail of her palomino. She was riding a plum-colored silver-studded rig to knock your eye out. The old boys in the Moon-Dog bunkhouse when I was a boy would have called her a peach, and kissed their fingertips. The Mosley boys whistled and hooted, though I told them she wouldn't remember us since we'd never even met her, only seen her once working her well-trained skinny horse. I didn't bother to remind them how I'd once known the girl's mother.

The celebrity parade had more gorgeous horses and saddles, more fringed and spangled clothing than I'd seen in forever. There was some spectacular handcrafted leather and silver work, saddles with oak leaves and acorns, some with eagles and mule deer bucks and does, some with cactus and desert wildlife, sidewinders, roadrunners, scorpions. I thought I even recognized a few of these old saddles on new mounts, from back when my grandad and father rode the Switzer parade up front with the big dogs, in their spotless white Stetsons and shiny black alligator boots. I knew from the Moon Dog's tack room how these fancy rigs gathered dust most of the year, and only got polished up for a rare sunshine ride like today. But with their glory gleaming through the mists of time, they were still an eyeful.

One thing the boys caught right away was how many Native Americans were in the parade, with handwoven blankets over their saddles, with their eagle-feather headdresses, beaded leggings and moccasins. When Ike asked if they were entered in events, I had to say I wasn't sure. There were lots more Native Americans here than there'd been when I was a boy. Mo had spotted three tipis set up out in front of the county fairgrounds, and said he wouldn't mind seein' what they had goin' on in there.

The announcer recited the names of those in the parade, and the rodeo sponsors, then listed the events for the day, and with that we were underway. I unpacked a couple pair of binoculars for us to share for the first event, which was barrel racing. I told the boys I'd found that girl's name in the program. She was Mazy DeVoss. Her mother had been a fine roper and barrel racer I'd seen compete way back when as Hetty DeVoss. It said Mazy would be fourth to run. The boys were tickled that this first event was all girls, and quickly caught on to the rules. Three barrels were set out in a cloverleaf pattern, and the contestants crossed the start and finish line for the run against the clock. If they knocked over a barrel they lost five seconds, that effectively meant they finished out of the money, though they were allowed to put out a hand going by and tip the barrel back up if it was wobbling but hadn't yet hit the ground. I remembered as a boy thinking the first time I saw barrel racers ride with their hair streaming out from under their hat brims, that they must treat their horses' manes and tails with the same stuff they put on their own hair. So somehow this was not just about their speed rounding barrels, nor the sprinting between, but about grace and allure that included their flowing hair, some kind of romantic display or courting ritual, all chase and no capture. Once in a while a girl contrived to lose her hat just as she spun the third barrel and broke for the line, that lent a bright flash to the finish. I don't think I ever saw a short-haired girl win a barrel race, though I didn't tell that to Ike and Mo. I did say sometimes a boy competed on barrels, but never saw one beat the girls.

So we watched the barrel riders stretch out and twirl their ponies round the course. The first made a solid run but swung wide on two turns. The second turned tighter and a shade faster than the first. The third girl crowded the first barrel and it teetered and toppled though she ran the rest of the course without a hitch. Then it was Mazy's turn. I warned the boys that she couldn't do a thing but run and turn like all the other girls. But she had changed her outfit, wasn't riding the palomino and fancy rig she'd had in the parade, but a tight little saddle on a plain brown gelding, stocky and sure-footed, that looked to be pure quarter horse. I spotted a sprig of lavender in the band of her wide brown hat, but that was it by way of filagree. This would be serious business.

She looped around in the warmup area, then lifted the reins and her horse shot like a rocket through the ankle-high photocell to start the run. The boys were shocked at how fast her horse took off. Then it was one right turn around the first barrel, then two lefts and the gallop home to stop the clock. Clean as a whistle, Ike said. She had shaved a full second off the second girl's run, and was easily the best so far, in under 13 seconds.

The fifth girl had a little more bling than the others, a strawberry blonde in a red outfit with long white fringes everywhere. But rounding the first barrel her pony stumbled. She slid from her seat and landed hard. Her horse scrambled up wild-eyed and fled, circling the arena, frantic to find a way out of there. But the girl bounded right up too, smiled and waved to show she was all right, then caught up her big white hat, dusted it off and set it back where it belonged. By then somebody else had galloped out and caught her horse, that drew a smatter of applause.

After that they brought out a tractor to fluff up and even out the dirt, and reset the barrels with measurements off some fence posts. Only three more contestants ran the course, one of them a raven-haired Comanche girl, a strong rider on a pony she'd dabbed two red handprints onto its rump for the push, which was the right idea, but the pony could have used a little more hustle and muscle. And that was it, the announcer declared Mazy DeVoss the winner. The boys whistled and hooted and jumped up and down. There was a lull before the next event, so I said Why don't you boys go say hello to Mazy, and congratulate her. She might like to hear how you remember her from that O'Grady's auction where we saw her first. She's a pretty fine horse trainer, so maybe you could pick up a tip or two. You boys look like you been around, and might have a little to talk about, if she's got a minute.

All at once they fell silent, stricken with shyness, but I gave 'em a grin, passed them a few bucks for cokes or ice cream and off they went. By then the gates and chute were set up for calf roping and tying. I settled in to watch the mounted cowboy chase the calf from the chute, toss a loop over it, dismount and catch the calf, throw it down, slip his piggin' string onto one foot, twirl it around two other feet, drop a half-hitch on the end and throw up his hands to stop the clock. These boys needed a good horse that would hold and back steady, keep the rope taut and the calf from gettin' loose. There were a lotta moving parts to this little dance. The first cowboy chased and dandled his loop too slow, and by the time his hands shot up the clock said 19 seconds. The second cowboy was a solid roper but his calf had been yanked off its feet by his horse, so he had to pick it up and throw it down again, which made his run about 16 and a half.

The third cowboy missed his throw and got no time at all. As the fourth roper was set to start his run, Ike and Mo showed up. I grinned and pointed, and they slipped in beside me to watch. This cowboy got a clean short toss, brought the calf up easy, slid out of the saddle and tossed the calf down, then tied the calf with his piggin' string all a blur, and shot his hands up. His time was eleven seconds and change. And all at once everyone was on their feet for this cowboy who'd made it look easy.

When we were finished clapping and sat back down, I asked if the boys had found Mazy. They both grinned and said they sure had. Mo said she looks even better up close, and she was still sittin' her plain brown horse that we told her was the best. Ike said she had a couple of girlfriends and a couple of boyfriends there, that were all horse and cow people, and didn't mind us. Then her mother Hetty showed up, and her younger brother Andy, who's 11, just like Mo. They found out Mazy was 16 now, the youngest barrel rider entered today, and would win some real prize money. They told about when they saw Mazy selling that skinny mare that she rode in blindfold, that took a bow at the end, and she said she remembered them cheering. Her mother had asked if they rode horses too, and it turned out they knew all about you, how you always had good horses, and good water on your place, which made me laugh for some reason. Ike looked up at me and said What? I said Nobody likes mud in their water, man nor horse. Besides, what with all their trick ponies, they got no room to talk.

By the time they'd finished telling me all the Mazy goings-on, we'd missed a couple more calf ropers, but nothing spectacular. They also said on the way back they had ducked into those tipis out front. In one there was a Native woman with long braids cooking what she called "kneel-down bread" in a big skillet and serving it to her five little kids with a big pot of beans and rice and sweet peppers. Mo said She gave us each a piece, with some beans and rice on it, that tasted just like you make. But we had no time for culinary niceties, since right away Mo asked me Why do calf ropers tie three feet together, 'stead of four? I said Good question. I expect the rules say "any three feet" so you don't have to think about it, and the calf stays just as still, but calmer than it would with four feet tied. Or so the old-timers thought. It's been done that way forever. Besides, tying all four feet the winner might just be the cowboy with the biggest hands. I said In this event you get one throw, one chance to do it right, that's it. Some of it you can't help. But I will tell you one new thing I've seen. What's that, they said in unison. I said This afternoon I've seen a couple left-handed ropers jump off the right side of their horse to avoid getting caught in their own rope.

The next event was team roping, with two cowboys on horseback, a header and a heeler. I told the boys how the one settled a loop on the steer's head or horns, then the other caught the steer by the hind legs, or heels. The clock stopped when the two horses had stretched the steer out and were both facing him. I pointed how this event worked a full-grown steer, about how it's still done on big outfits, where a large animal might need to be caught to be branded or doctored, that would be a handful for one cowboy to manage. The roping had to be deft, with only one shot for each cowboy. And you got a penalty if the header only caught one horn, or the heeler only caught one hind foot.

We settled in and watched the rest of the team roping. After a while I asked the boys if they noticed anything about the horses they were using. Yeah, said Ike, they're all big an' heavy. An' tall. I said Good eye, then pointed out how most of them were using roping saddles, with a low cantle and a much thicker horn, to take the stress involved in working big steers. The boys thought these teams looked more like real workin' cowboys, with their gear a little more worn and dirty. And Ike said It was hard to follow some of that rope work with your eye, when the fastest teams could head and heel and stretch out a steer in eight or nine seconds flat.

Then came steer wrestling. While they were getting set up, I mentioned a couple things--that all these steers had horns, and the steer wrestlers all had a teammate, a mounted hazer on the far side of the steer, to keep him in line. And that this was a competition for the biggest strongest cowboys. Mo said How come? I said because they have to grab a full-grown steer by the horns, eight or nine hundred pounds, wrestle him to the ground, and twist his head till all four feet are in the air. I wanted the boys to see and understand it all, but figured maybe I shouldn't talk so much, just let the show have its say.

About then the first steer came running out, with the hazer on his left, and the wrestler on his right. The cowboy leaned down and slid off his horse at a gallop, grabbed the steer's horns, dug in his heels and twisted the steer's head a half turn till his nose was pointing to the sky. It seemed to take forever till the steer flopped over and stuck his four feet in the air. Then the cowboy picked up his hat and gave a little nod to the round of applause.

Mo said it looked like the cowboy might break the cow's neck. I said these steers are awful tough. I've never seen one hurt getting wrestled. The announcer gave the time, 10.49 seconds. The next cowboy was much bigger, but not so athletic. When he caught up with the steer, leaned low, grabbed at the horns and jumped, the steer ducked and shook his head, and slipped out from under the cowboy, who toppled face-first in the dirt, and came up sputtering.

None of the other steer wrestlers missed the horns, though there were some furious tussles. Some steers were harder than others to get off their feet, and even down some just didn't want to put their feet in the air. There were three cowboys who were so smooth and dominant they seemed in another league from the rest of the competitors. And the times showed it: those three had times around 8-10 seconds, while the rest had times from 16 to over 20 seconds.

After Steer Wrestling came Wild Cow Milking. The announcer named the ranches that had sent teams of 4 for this event. The Moon-Dog had sent a team those years back when I was a boy, but no more. There were two mounted ropers, and two cowboys on foot. The judge came out and painted a six-foot circle of whitewash in the dirt near the grandstand. The wild cow would be let in on the far side of the arena, and the two mounted ropers would chase the cow until one of them dropped a loop on her. Then the two cowboys on foot would run up and get hold of the cow. The biggest one who held the cow's head was called the mugger, and he was given a hand by the cowboy who had missed with his lasso, while the milker would move in. Sometimes it took all four of them on foot, before one could reach in and squirt a little milk into a dented aluminum bottle. When the milker thought he had enough milk, he would run with the bottle to the white-wash circle, and stop the clock.

At that point the judge would ride to the circle, lean down and take the bottle, and if enough of a dribble of white came out when he poured, he'd pronounce it Milk or else No milk. The thing is, none of these wild cows had ever been milked, and most would rather jump over the moon than have some hamfisted cowboy handle their udder. One cow had to have the two biggest cowboys on her head mugging her, and the third cowboy pulling her tail while the last one tried to reach in and milk her. I pointed out how these cowboys mostly had their old everyday hats on. Which told you they might likely get brushed off and stepped on, with all this foolish-ness going on. Despite all the laughter and hooting, this seemed the hardest event on the cowboys so far, and I asked the boys why that was. Mo said 'Cause she don't want to give 'em no milk. When I said Why not? he said 'Cause it belongs to her baby.

After that came the two horseback bucking events, bareback and saddle bronc riding. In both events the cowboy had to ride eight seconds to the buzzer. Bareback broncs were leaner, from a hundred to near two hundred pounds lighter, and the rider had to hold on with one hand to a girth strap with a leather handle. Because of how the horse bucked, the rider would lean back and recline along the horse's back, and spur the bronc along his chest and shoulders. Mounts were chosen by lots, though the horse got half the score, up to 50 points, for the quality of his bucking, and the rider got the other half, up to another 50 points, for his riding and spur-ring and other cowboy moves. Your spare hand was supposed to be waving in the air. You could be disqualified if you used it to touch the horse or your other hand or even scratched your nose.

The saddle bronc rider had a saddle with stirrups, and a single heavy woven rope attached to the horse's halter. Both bareback and saddle broncs used a bucking strap padded inside with wool that ran under the horse's belly, just ahead of the hind legs. While we were waiting for the first bareback bronc riders to come out, the boys asked if these horses would buck without the strap. I said You bet they would. These horses were chosen to buck, and like to buck. Some are saddle horses that got ruined, that never would trust a rider.

Ike said he thought riding bareback broncs and saddle broncs were both like driving a car with no steering wheel. Mo said And no brakes. More than half of the bronc riders didn't make it to the buzzer, lost the rhythm of their waving and spurring, heaving back and forth till they lost their seat and slipped off or went flying. The riders who got tossed stumbled after their hats and limped off. The riders who made it to the buzzer stuck around to let the crowd get a look at them as they smiled and waved to friends, and savored the moment.

After the bronc riding events the announcer said there'd be an intermission for supper, and as the sun was going down we were feeling peckish, so went and got some ribs and beans and lemonade and a slice of pie, and brought our cardboard platters and plastic forks back to our seats so we wouldn't miss a thing. But I had forgotten something Ike and Mo noticed as soon as we got back. The last event of the evening was going to be bull riding, the roughest rodeo event, the most dangerous, and the one that I'da skipped if there had been any way of the boys not catching on. But I shoulda had more faith in 'em, because right away what they saw were the clowns.

As Ike said, They're just like circus clowns, with red noses, crazy face paint and lipstick, only one was a barrel clown and the other two were bullfighter clowns. They all wore cowboy hats, and all three had their pants hacked off just below the knees, and wore what looked like stout lace-up boots, that I bet had steel toes. Under their loud suspenders and checkered shirts they wore the same kind of padded vest bull-riders wore, that made them look plump where they weren't. I told the boys I'd known a couple rodeo clowns who were both firemen. I said Think about it, the kinda guys who run into burning buildings to save folks, who every summer put on this silly getup and spend their vacation doing rodeos like this, to snatch up a cowboy so he don't get stepped on or gored once he's down. I didn't need to describe what they did or how they did it, all we had to do was sit there and watch the first cowboy, Clyde Ames, come out of gate 1 on Fool Me Twice. He had on a helmet with a hockey mask, and wore short fringed chaps that showed off his spurring. The bull only made three or four spectacular spiraling leaps, then the cowboy was down, and the three clowns moved in. The barrel clown rolled himself and the big blue barrel out between the bull and Clyde, dodged and faked Fool Me Twice while one clown waved his red cape in the bull's face, as the other clown snatched the cowboy to his feet and dragged him off. Once the bull was shuffled and faked away to a holding pen, the clowns and Clyde all skipped up and took a bow. The audience went wild.

The next bull, named Medium Rare, sunfished, jumped up and swapped end for end in a way no horse ever could, which finally tossed the rider with a couple seconds to go. Poor Lester Winton musta been pretty dizzy, flew off like a rag doll and landed so hard the clowns really had to work to keep the bull off him till he came to, looked up and blinked like a turtle. That blue barrel got butted halfway across the arena with the clown inside, though he came up honking a horn at the bull. One of the clowns had the bull by the tail, digging in his heels to slow him down, while the other clown lifted Lester and dragged him out through the gate.

The first bull that got ridden to the buzzer was Dead On Arrival, a good-sized Brahma-Hereford cross with straight horns and a mean look in his eye. Ike asked me why this rider had a cowboy hat on, instead of the helmet with a hockey mask the others wore. I said I think 'cause he's older, maybe started riding bulls before they made the helmet rule, and got grand-fathered in. The rider Micah Reedy came out of the chute with a steady rocking motion that seemed to help him keep his seat, not go flying while the crafty bull tried to fishtail and slide out from under. When the buzzer sounded, the clowns closed in to catch him as he slid off. But then things turned ugly, and Micah was shaken around like a scarecrow spittin' straw. He couldn't let go, his fingers were caught in the rigging on the bull strap between the bull's shoulders. One of the clowns ducked around behind the bull and climbed up his other side to untangle the braided line wrapped around Micah's hand. It was a tricky move that only took a heartbeat, all the while the bull kept jumping and the two men kept jumping with it on either side. It seemed like forever before the cowboy's hand was freed and the bull got distracted and lured away. The clowns put his hat on Micah, all hunched over, hugging his right hand close, and helped him hobble out to wild applause.

That was the best ride we saw. The boys wanted to know if that old cowboy Micah Reedy broke anything. I said I didn't know, he mighta dislocated a couple of fingers or his wrist, that the doctors could pop back in place but might hurt and take a while to mend. The boys saw how each bull had a little different dance, that the cowboy had only a couple jumps to get in time and tune with, before they parted company. We saw another five or six bulls and riders. A big pale yellow bull balanced on his front feet and threw his head way back, a move that could head-butt the rider if he happened to get thrown up over the bull's shoulders. Another mean-looking brindle bull would jump so high on his hind legs that the rider slid back-wards straight off the bull's butt. The last bull of the evening seemed to be able to jump up and twist his spine so his front end came down on his left foot while his rear end would land on his right foot, that flung the rider off sideways. So we only saw that one rider hold on till the buzzer and win a prize.

Then the announcer bid us one and all good night, and we flowed with the crowd to the parking lot and sat in the truck with the windows down listening to the crickets and peepers and whatnot, while we let the traffic clear out. We all set quiet a little, then I asked What was the best name for a bull you heard today? Ike said Hot Mess, and Mo said Bandersnatch, that got us laughin'. They wanted to know my favorite, and I said Flapdoodle, which Mo said wasn't even a bull but a buckin' bronc. I said My head is so fulla names I could hardly say which one was which.

We got to talkin' about bucking horses. Mo said they didn't seem so bad, maybe they'd even be nice if you didn't try to ride one. They looked big and strong, and both boys still wondered what got the horses to buck. I said What else but to get rid of something they can't stand on their backs. They buck naturally, and quit once it's gone or else they decide they can't shake it off no matter what. They're smart so mostly try somehow to get along. The bucking strap around their belly is sort of a reminder, that aggravates 'em just enough to try an' shake it loose. And Ike said, So you think they're in on the show? I said Maybe. The strap's only on for a minute or two, and the rider is on a few seconds, unless he's real lucky, or sticks like glue.

When we were done laughing, Mo said Bareback bronc riders look like they're trying to take a nap, stretched out along the horse's back, only the horse wouldn't let 'em. The riders were just hanging onto the belly band with one hand between their legs, like the horse was a leather barrel fulla Mexican jumping beans. Ike said Saddle bronc riders looked a little more like they're really tryin' to ride the horse, though they didn't even have reins, just that one braided lead to the halter. So they're just along for the ride too, though the saddle makes you think they might stick.

Then I asked what did they think of the bulls? Ike allowed as how they were too dangerous--so much muscle that looked sleepy but was all wound up, set to explode. I said What makes you say that? He said How they kick and heave around behind the gate. They're mad before they even come out. He said he was afraid for the cowboys. A bull could jump up and swap ends before he came down. He could jump up and just about kick the top of his own head with one hind foot. How could you stay on top of that?

I said Bulls aint so bad on the ranch. Though they can be pushy on their home range. Impatient and irritable. But with a short attention span. So they mostly bluff and bluster, then forget.

I notice you don't have one.

That's right, Ike, not at the moment. I used to have a pretty good one, that we called Poppa Butter, 'cause he'd butt whatever got in his way. We mostly could get him to do what we wanted, when there wasn't a cow winkin' at him. But I had to sell him in that last dry spell some years back. Now I've got a deal with one of my neighbors that's been workin' pretty good. Sandy Perry is a little ascairt of his bull, so I help him work around it.

In exchange I haul my ladies over to his place for a little romance.

As we got out to the road and picked up speed for the long ride home, I told the boys that was the rodeo I'd watched as a boy. Some of the rules have changed, and there's more professional cowboys than there once was, though most we saw today were still local boys and girls. Mo said how could you tell? I said By their last names that are still mostly the same old families. Although I had to admit I hadn't been back there once since I was seventeen. Mo said Why not? I said I didn't know where I was going then, except away from here. I went in the Army straight out of school, when all I knew was working horses and cattle. Which the Army had none of. But then they taught me to take orders, shoot straight and stay outa trouble.

Finally I asked what they thought of the cowhands. Did they seem like regular cowboys and cowgirls? Ike said How could we tell? I said Did they seem like they'd done regular chores on a regular place--mucked out stalls, fed chickens, patched fence? Ike thought about it a minute, then said Not so much. Still, both the boys were impressed, said they did better than anybody might expect. Ike said from what he'd seen on TV he thought rodeo cowboys might be like acrobats, some kinda performers who didn't do all that ranch stuff. I said You're thinkin' they're some kinda specialists? Ike said Yeah, like they only do the one thing over and over, till they get it right. Mo said And they hafta beat the clock! We all thought about that for a minute.

After a while Mo leaned back and sagged and fell asleep. As the truck rumbled and droned on, I asked Ike Does the rodeo make you want to be a cowboy?

Yes, he said, a little. If I could find something that I did just right.

I said When I was a boy they still had these little tent circuses that traveled around, set up and did a few shows, then tore down and were gone. And for years out in the country, kids would want to run away and join the circus. And once in a while someone did.

Yeah, he said, but a rodeo's different. Like you said this morning, a rodeo belongs to a place and the folks that live around there. It's like they're playing these games for each other, and themselves.

Games made out of work?

Yeah, I guess. But games somebody you know might be good at.

After a lull Ike said One thing, I think cowboys behave different when there's more people around than animals. I said Different? He said Yeah, different, and maybe not so good.

I said I had to agree. But there's lots of silliness cowhands can get in their heads since they spend so much time off on their own. Then I had a thought, something those left-handed ropers reminded me of. I told Ike about a cowhand I knew who'd switch sides climbing onto his horse every time, so he wouldn't stretch out the leather and make his left stirrup longer, since he'd say It stands to reason if you put all your weight climbing up on the left side, the right side won't stretch out as much. I could only think how his horse musta felt around other horses when this bird half the time climbs up him on the wrong side. And how does a thick buckled harness strap even count in such logic? Most cowboys never changed their stirrups from the day they bought the saddle and first tossed it up on a horse till the day they needed a hand to climb a horse that last time, and to look at their stirrups, most stayed perfectly level. It stands to reason a horse can get used to just about anything, even a nutcase worried about stretching leather. Long as you keep your seat and your sense of humor, you'll be fine.

There was no more to be said till we pulled into his parents' yard and turned the truck around, then I reached back to nudge Mo awake and help him up. Ike said You mind if I go out to the barn with you an' see are the horses all right? If that's what you're gonna do. And I said Sure, since he was right, it was just what I had in mind after a long day gone.

After we parked the truck by my house and went crunching along in the dark to the barn I said You mind tellin' me why you want a look around? Ike said Maybe I just need reminding there's critters leadin' good lives, that don't ever get messed with. And he was lookin' up and nodding as I said Never did an' never would.

A Likely Spot From Here On Out

Recently I've been sitting around wondering if I'd about run out
of moves on the old home place. Thumbing through my notebook, looking over plans I'd been making since the last drought, that for a while had
seemed like a master plan. At first I'd had no plan at all, beyond keeping
a little extra money on hand for hard times, that really just came out of
talking things over that one morning with Claude Ferryman down at Ferryman Farm Supply. I'd been picking up some calf feed and we'd been shootin'
the breeze on how the cost of living just went one way up. Seemed like there
was no way to keep prices down anywhere near what a body workin' away
on their own could afford. Our talk had started when I noticed the price
of calf medicines and feed had just gone up again. That and vet bills were
way beyond the market price for beef on the hoof, so every sick calf same
as meant a loss. The price of land had crept up too, to where a body could
hardly dream of a place of their own anymore. When I'd got home later
I had sat on the porch in the rocker beside a big glass of iced tea with its
sweat soaking into the boards, while I thought things through.

And what I'd been looking at that afternoon and ever since was
the front of the place, straight out the gravel drive to the crossroads. After
a while I'd gone out to the barn, saddled Beulah, and rode the place top to
bottom, side to side and end to end, slow and quiet, while that mare helped
focus my thoughts, nodding everywhere I turned, nodding everywhere we
stopped to take a look. By the time I got back to the house I'd had the idea I
might be able to plot out eleven lots on the northeast side along the county
road, and not miss it much. It was scrubby hillside pasture that had always
needed more water and manure than what it ever got.

Lucky for me, those first land-shoppers I'd met had been Clint and
Eva Mosley, though I hadn't chanced to meet their two little boys just yet.
It was a Wednesday evening, one of those long slow August sunsets, two

days after I'd taken out the ad in three shopping newspapers all printed in English and Spanish, by the same outfit, the only such papers that made it to every mailbox for two hundred miles around. Maybe I just craved to take the measure of my neighbors. This attractive steady young couple drove up in an old pickup with a contractor's pipe rack up over the bed. We'd shook hands on the porch and I'd poured them some iced tea and after a while asked their business. They wanted a look at the land I had for sale, that I was glad to show them. Clint had been framing houses for a contractor I knew in town, Ed Grimes, and said he'd learned just enough to be dangerous, and was about set to build them a place of their own and quit paying rent. We'd walked up the drive and over to where the lots were staked out along the road. The prices weren't bad, if I do say, and they knew it and I knew it, and they looked just about set to reach in their pockets by the time we'd done talking well-drilling, septic, drain fields, power poles and such.

I had hired a surveyor to lay out those eleven square three-acre lots in a row along the road, keeping the crossroads corner lot for myself. I'd set the prices low enough that I figured to find out what kind of neighbors some of my own dirt might make. I thought the ad made it pretty clear where it said "Owner-built only, no developers." When the first lots sold right away, for a while it had got noisy and busy with building, though my house and barn were at least a quarter-mile off. I had run a good fence along the inside of my pasture down that one side, but while there was building going on I kept my livestock away from the noise and mess, nail guns, compressors and the like.

The building had mostly gone pretty quick, since most of the buyers were young, set to push hard and get on with their lives. Clint Mosley built his mostly by himself, though Eva knew how to lend a hand without making a fuss and kept their two boys out from underfoot, and I gave him a hand lifting, tossing up piles of sheathing and shingles, lining up rafters and such. And all the noise and bustle of building appeared to draw others this way, so it didn't take long to sell the rest. Still, there were surprises. The Danziger brothers, Bert and Larry, for example, hadn't believed in nail guns, and pounded every single nail home—which I couldn't help but find refreshing, though after a few days the sound of it did start to nag at me.

After all, it was where my bad elbow had come from, building and fencing back before power tools.

Ever since I'd sold the ten of those eleven lots--and had to buy one back, plus its ramshackle house and capped oil well, for the time being rented out--I'd been feeling my way toward something, but wasn't sure what. Somewhere back inside I started to feel somehow that what I'd got myself caught up in, like it or not, was really community. And mostly found I liked it, especially once I'd made friends with the Mosleys and their boys. It wasn't just nice to have somebody else tangled up in my days, it had me thinkin' and doin' and mindin' other folks, what they needed and cared about, without so much gab and guff about my own self.

And ever since that first year, I'd been doing a little something up at the crossroads, near where my driveway turns off the state route. Every year I'd picked out and done a thing or two off my list. I'd started by moving my big homemade picnic table off the concrete pad where I'd set it with Clint's help, out to the corner of the crossroads, centered about fifty feet in from the road. Then I'd planted six red maple trees, in two groups of three on either side, where they'd throw shade over that corner of the ranch --and over that stout picnic table big enough for dinner for ten or twelve--during the heat of the day. I'd been oiling that table too, a couple times a year, so it would last a while. Then I'd fenced in the trees so the deer couldn't eat 'em to nothing before they jumped up out of reach and got their growth. The third year I'd had a couple good loads of gravel dumped on that corner and spread it out nice and even, then built a stout hitching post by the table, where the other trees threw their shade, so the boys and I could stop there, tie up our horses and eat our lunch, and watch the folks driving by. Actually I was thinkin' that at some point other folks out along the two roads might take a ride this way, and likely need a place and patch of shade inviting enough to climb down, set a while and catch their breath.

So I'd made a start. In the most recent year I'd pulled the fence in off the corner on both sides, so someone besides us could use the shade and picnic table. And I put a gate in the new fence while I was at it. I talked to the highway people and got a couple long pieces of culvert set in each ditch, that I dumped gravel over and tamped down so cars and trucks could pull in there.

After that for a few months every other day I'd go out and park myself at the table, just look around awhile and see what else it might need. From that angle I could admire the ten lots in a row with their homemade houses in various stages of finish, that reached from a little below the northeast corner of my place down an easy hill so that all the new neighbors had a view out over the widest part of my land to the south and west. They could also see what was straight across the crossroads from where I set, a patch of weeds that had never been known as anything but Buddy's Corners, though he only owned the one. The land across from mine was pretty flat, and that land owner old Buddy Dwyer and his friends had been in the habit of parking tractors and farm implements and backhoes, old cars and such with for-sale signs, phone numbers and prices, on that corner where folks going by all four ways had to stop anyhow. Buddy took a small cut of each sale for the advertising. And for as long as I'd had the place that's all there'd ever been, apart from the four big stop signs. Practically the only time we saw a sheriff's deputy out this way was when one or another had had such a slow shift they needed to write them some tickets, so backed away into the weeds, set to catch whatever lazy clown come blazin' through.

I hadn't said a thing to Buddy Dwyer about the little improvements on my side facing his, since all we ever did for years was wave. If he'da come over and asked, I'da told him what I was thinkin'. But whatever I was doing, I was just taking it as easy as you please. On one of the pages of my spiral-bound notebook where I gathered the notions and daydreams that sometimes turned into plans, I had jotted down a few things under the heading of crossroads that I knew right away were some kind of a wish list. I had written down a small general store, and under that one-day-a-week farmer's market. Below that was No gas station! and No church! Not that I minded either establishment, but if there was only room for one and I had to choose among all the different kinds, I'd rather there be none to avoid the noise and squabble. And the last items so far: sandwiches, cold pop and coffee. Was that about the size of it? What was this gonna be anyhow, the start of a town, an unincorporated village? By now there were seventeen people living in those ten houses, plus myself and Reynaldo and Clyde, the two old cowboys that were still campin' in my bunkhouse and fending for themselves. Twenty in all at the moment, plus four or five more neighbors within walking distance, say half a mile. Enough that every day someone might need a roll of toilet paper, a loaf of bread, a can of juice or a dozen eggs. Small stuff, not worth the half-hour drive to town, but needed just the same.

I had to admit when the deals were all signed, then in short order all the hammering and sawing had commenced, I'd had a moment of doubt. It had felt like these strangers were watchin' me, and some of 'em couldn't help but be nosey and opinionated, maybe not so contemplative as country folk are rumored to be, and I might not have paid enough attention to who I was selling what had begun feeling like parts of myself. I'd picked this place because it was halfway between a couple sleepy towns that might stay small. But it felt like even here out on the edge, the world was filling up, and starting to crowd me a little.

But when I'd sat and thought it out, I realized that you can't really pick your neighbors. All you get are first impressions, and appearances can be deceiving, so your choice is really to be neighborly or not, and see how things developed.

So I studied and kept at it. I bought a heavy new galvanized garbage can, and painted it green, with masking tape spelled out GARBAGE, that came through in shiny letters once I peeled away the tape. I also got some chain, and padlocked it and the lid to the picnic table so it wouldn't wander off in some of the stout winds and urges we get.

So what would this turn out to be--a village, even in time a small town? For the rancher in me, the crossroads was plenty, with four directions to choose from, four ways outa here. But that also meant four ways in, through and away. Any kind of settlement could easily get too noisy and cluttered for my horses and cows. I'd been glad when the hammering on those ten houses was done, and the quiet pretty much returned. Then I ran into one answer. When I saw we might need a little store, I started sketching it out, how much counter and how many shelves, how much refrigeration, what kind of a stove--all that sorta thing. But then one morning I called out Whoa, pulled back the reins and called a halt. I realized I didn't want to run it or even make money off it. I just saw the need for a little store to be here, and wanted to help it come to life. But maybe I had put the cart before the horse. I reckoned maybe I needed to find the right person, or better, the place needed to find that right person, then let him or her see what they needed instead. That day I suspected this was what some folks called growing up, that others just called growing old. But I did start to see I wasn't the center of anything hereabouts, and didn't need to be.

For a while I wondered what it was that had stopped me, that I couldn't seem to see again. What had turned me around? I remember that day I'd gone out to the barn, thinking to saddle up Beulah for another ride. And today was a brisk fall morning when I walked out that way again, trying to retrace my steps and figure what it had been that brought me to a screechin' halt. I rubbed Beulah on the neck and shoulder, and gave her an apple, the last one I had left around the place. Then all at once I looked up and saw again what it was I'd seen. Those forty-foot steel I-beams that spanned the barn, that Bernie and Annalee had somehow got in there, just how they'd never said, so they'd have this huge clear open space. They'd made this place an airplane hangar, and had a runway on the flattest piece of ground. And they'd paid for it all in haircuts, a snip at a time. Now here I called what I was doing ranchin', and hadn't made use of a thing they had done. The ambition and splendor and subtlety of it shamed me. I could empty out the box stalls and most all the stuff I'd made, and I could have an indoor riding ring for when it was too hot or cold to work outside. Forty by sixty feet, this great big space could be used for lots of other things. The upstairs was warm and snug, with a nice tight roof and floor, and could be used for a workshop or school, classrooms or an indoor playground.

What hit me was how folks mostly make their lives out of parts of other lives, especially if someone leaves them a toehold, a start of something unfinished for the next generation to work on. A place to begin again. We don't always need to tear a thing down when its first use is done, and build it all over from scratch. Even the crossroads here had just been waitin' for a chance when the right person might stop to take a look around, and see something talking to them. So unless that was me, maybe my part was at an end.

Then it wasn't a week later when Lucille and Floyd Munro stepped up on the porch one afternoon and wanted to talk. They'd built the fourth house, a nice solid bungalow, and had started gardening, and mostly due to Lucille it had gotten way out of hand, till now they were growing two acres of vegetables and a dozen fruit trees. I had figured what they wanted to talk about was some kind of trade for manure. But what they really wanted to know was could they use my big picnic table out on the corner lot on Saturdays from next spring through fall, for a little farmer's market. And though spring was still way the other side of Thanksgiving and Christmas, I said Sure, why not, but better paint you a nice big sign.

Hat Christmas

That Christmas the Mosleys gave me a big white hat that musta cost 'em a fortune, with a hard case you could prit'near park a truck on. When I put it on and looked in the mirror it just about hurt my eyes. I already had a nice enough black cowboy hat for dress-up and a battered gray one for work, and both of 'em fit and suited me fine for most jobs, where I wouldn't feel bad to be seen around town or on the place. But the boys said now everybody would know I was one of the good guys. Both of 'em liked how it made me look, and so did Eva and Clint. When I put it on the first time they stood in a row and all gave me the thumbs-up. Which stopped me, made me wonder what it was they were seeing, that I couldn't quite see for myself.

The boys got a couple new cowboy hats too, not their usual straw but real felt ones, not so fancy as mine but lookin' mighty grownup, that would keep the sun and rain off. At 12 and 11 they were gettin' pretty grownup too. Clint and Eva had talked to me a couple times about it all, after the boys were in bed. Before Christmas they'd started off askin' me what I looked for in a hat, and heard me say No holes, and looked puzzled, till I said in a pinch you want to be able to give your horse a drink, dip the thing in the river or fill from a stock tank or garden hose, so no grommets or vents in the sides that'll dribble water down your pants. But that was just for starters. Soon they had some good hard questions, wanted to know what I thought of this whole gift-giving business, and how they ought to try to sneak up on it.

I said it was about loving and belonging, that wasn't just giving, it was giving and receiving, that was not quite as simple as give-and-take. We were sitting out around their fire pit on a cool night, with some blankets over us, and a couple logs blazing. I shared an old answer, one I'd used for myself since I was in grade school. I said Imagine a box that you cut a hole in the bottom of, and stuck your hand up inside, then closed the top and held it out to someone. If they opened it, and didn't take your hand, they wouldn't take you, so there was no point putting a gift in the box. If they thought you were a fool, or crazy, there was no point either. A gift was a way of giving a little of yourself.

But then there were people who could give gifts but didn't know how to receive one. My Grampa had been one of those. He had pretty much one of everything, and sometimes would give fancy presents, but then he didn't like to unwrap a gift from someone else, even on his own birthday or Christmas, even from some little kid he saw around every day. He'd try to avoid it. It took me till I was in my twenties to see the obvious answer, that he was lacking something we call self-respect. And he couldn't see that receiving a gift was a skill and a gift in itself. People didn't give you things to clutter up your life, though that might seem to be the effect. Beyond a certain point if you were a grownup you got things for yourself, and mostly had what you needed to go about living your life. But friends and their love could help you with more than the clutter.

One thing you could do with folks who had everything, was give them something that'll disappear. A pie or nice bottle of wine, or even snow tires. Something that'll be eaten or drunk up or worn out before long. One thing people did gift-giving was get lazy, and start giving someone the same thing over and over. My grandma who I never met was one of those that people decided sometime way back when liked hummingbirds, because of course she did. She put out those feeders with yellow plastic flowers and red juice that they could hover and sip on through the winter. So people started giving her hummingbirds to hang on the wall, ones made out of stained glass, or painted on canvas, or printed on aprons. Hummingbird jewelry, pins and pendants and earrings. The old home place was still full of hummingbirds forty years after she died. I asked my dad once if she collected 'em, and he said You gotta be kiddin' me. She said she'd only liked to look at the real thing out the window on a winter day, that was plenty. I said Then why don't you get rid of 'em? Dad said Your Grampa's gettin' soft in the head, says he likes how they bring her to mind.

But then another thought for gift-giving was play, and there were still a few things that might help you remember to play, that should be part of life too. Because life is not all work, even if it can feel that way for weeks or months at a time, when you're stuck in the middle of something you have to get done. So at just the wrong moment say someone gives you a windup toy, that says play, that might feel like an insult to the serious grownup spot you're in, getting that old roof torn off and the new one on before the rains come.

But what else could life be, besides work and play? Sure, it could be love and passion, family and sharing. And what that meant all together in one place, which was belonging. Which meant safety and comfort, the feel of being home.

But then gifts could involve keeping a good secret, and building a good surprise. Some people hate both, and I've often wondered why. Mostly surprises come from outside, from events that are unplanned, sometimes accidents. Some changes that can't be helped, some threats that can't be avoided or planned for or against. And with the looming threats around us, some people get fatalistic, won't wear their seatbelt because they hate living in constant fear. So they say It'll come or it won't, and I'll deal with it then, else before I know it my life'll be over and done. Which is a way some folks have of lettin' their rugged independence break the law for 'em and worsen the effect, all the while denyin' what they're doin' amounts to a slow-motion suicide.

Clint and Eva had to chew on that a minute. But I was not about to shut up right when I was on a roll. I said my theory was that joy mostly had to steal up on you unawares. Some people couldn't throw a party for themselves, because if they could see a happy moment coming, they might swerve and avoid it altogether. Anything unplanned might upset their apple cart. I told about a family reunion I'd gone to where everybody was asked to play cornhole together, and the signups were set for there to be kind of a family championship. I had thought it wouldn't work because the people who suggested it were of a certain age and they all spent their summers in the back yard tossing those beanbags onto those slanted little tables with a hole in the middle, between grilling out and drinking beer. But the surprise was on them. They didn't know how talented some of their relatives were, and it turned out to be exciting to lose a game they might have been sure they would win. If they hadn't been such good sports it might have turned ugly, but turned out to be grand. Turned out the winner was an old farmer who had never played before at all, though he'd thrown horseshoes by the ton.

Finally I asked Eva and Clint what were the favorite gifts they'd ever got. They looked at each other, then said Why don't we show you, and went in the house for a few minutes while I poked the fire and watched the sparks swirl up and get lost in the stars. Clint brought out a shoe box and handed it to me. He also brought out a flashlight. We waited till Eva came out too, with a littler box mostly hid by her fingers. Then Clint opened his box and said This is what the boys gave me the Christmas before we built the new house and moved out here. It was a plastic kit model of a cabin cruiser, a classic old wooden Chris-Craft. It was carefully put together, with no glue showing, but every plank on the hull seemed to be painted a little different shade and texture, like the boat had been made out of a dozen different kinds of trees. The decking was painted that way too, very carefully, with no drips or runs. It must have taken a bunch of tiny brushes, and many hours under a bright light, deciding which color to paint next. The painting of the boat felt dreamy, and realer than real, like someone was trying to say how it might have been made, if it had been a real boat.

I said Is this something you always wanted? Clint shook his head, said it's a total mystery. I'd taken them out fishing for the first time the summer before, rented a little aluminum kicker boat. We had a great day, though we only caught three little fish, with worms for bait. I made 'em wear orange lifejackets, and wore one myself, and we joked about us all looking like orange creamsicles, and when we came back to the dock, as luck would have it the bait shop had orange creamsicles in their freezer, so we sat on a bench at the dock and ate 'em together. Then on the ride home Ike asked me if we could go out in the ocean with that kinda boat. And I said No, we'd want a bigger one, a cabin cruiser where we could cook and sleep and be safe. Then he said What would we want that for? And I said

Out there we might catch a fish as big as the boat, so big we might have to tow it ashore with a rope.

I was just funnin' with 'em, but the boys went on and on about what it was like out in the ocean, and asked a hundred questions I had no notion how to answer. But their imaginations were running wide open, going a mile a minute. They had a great time telling Eva about our day, while I cleaned and breaded and cooked up our three little sunfish for supper. After that day they didn't talk so much with me about the ocean, probably because they'd already heard everything I knew, but they kept talking with each other about it, after they went to bed.

Then Clint said, One more thing. I'd like you to take a peek inside the boat, on the starboard side. He handed me the flashlight, and I turned it on. And on the dark brown side through the portholes there was a white outline of a fish with a wide mouth full of teeth, that could have been smiling or menacing, that reached from bow to stern. A little boy painting, but unmistakably a huge fish with its round staring eye. I looked up at him, smiled and shook my head.

What do you make of that?

That's what I was gonna ask you.

Well, Clint, if I was to guess, I'd say it's about containing the fear. You talked about catching a fish too big for the boat. Well, there you have it, a fish that's all the boat could handle and then some. A fish thirty to forty feet long, that might even sink the boat. And where else could it come from but that first fishing trip, and talking about the ocean on the way home? The gift is sharing the magic, dreaming big, but then containing it, doing something they could do, that says how they feel about you.

A big shadowy fish with a mouthful of teeth in the dark?

It's a dream fish. A big dream, way bigger than they are. That they wanted to take charge of and make real, so they gave it to you. So maybe it's a hope, that they'll always have you with them. I've got a question for you. How did you learn there was a fish inside?

I found it the day after Christmas. The sun was streaming in the window, for the first time in days. The sun was so bright I held it up to admire the paint job, the colors, and just happened to look inside. At first I thought they must have signed it, before they glued on the deck and super-structure.

They didn't say anything?

Not a word.

And when you found it, what did you do?

At supper I asked them what it meant. Mo talked about seeing that cartoon movie of Pinocchio, how Geppetto got swallowed up by a whale, and Pinocchio built a fire in the whale to make the whale sneeze and rescued them, and how the boys thought that might be a good idea, but might make it too scary. Ike said we thought it ought to make us feel safe when we're out at sea, listening to the big fish gurgle and splash through the water.

And what did you say to that?

What could I say but thank you.

Eva said And there you are, safe in their dreams.

After that we sat quiet awhile and poked the fire, There's no telling what kids will think of, then somehow stick it all together with the magic glue of the mind. Then I asked Eva what she had to show us. She handed us a little black fuzzy rectangular jewelry box. Inside there was a tiny aluminum telescope about two inches long. The eyepiece pulled out another three-quarters of an inch. In the dark it was hard to see anything through it, though we could tell how it worked in the firelight. Eva held it up to study the sliver of moon coming up, then said this was from her best friend in the second and third grade, Conchita Ruiz. She asked for the flashlight, and along the barrel we could see, carefully scratched in, the letters "EVA -- CVR."

What was the gift for?

It was our last day of school in third grade. Her parents weren't getting along, and Conchita was going to live with her grandparents, in Mexico City. We didn't think we'd see each other again. When we met, on the first day of second grade, she'd happened to sit behind me because her last name was next in the alphabet. My maiden name is Ross, and hers is Ruiz. But last names in Spanish-speaking countries are tricky. She really had two last names, her mother's and her father's, Vega and Ruiz. And her first name was really a nickname, that meant "little shell." Her real first name was

Concepcion, and referred to one of the attributes of the Virgin Mary, how she was conceived without sin. The next day I brought her my most prized possession, that I had found on vacation the year before, on the beach in Tampa Florida. It was a wentletrap, a fancy little seashell that I had put in a red velvet bag. I gave it to her, a little seashell for the little seashell, and that was it. From that day on we did everything together at school for two years. She came home from school for visits and sleep-overs. Her English was better than mine, so she tried to teach me Spanish, and it quickly got so we could chatter in Spanish and the grownups in my house could hardly catch a word. Of course in her house we chattered in English, which her father and mother had mastered, but precisely and slowly, and their housekeeper and gardener knew only a few words, so mostly our secrets were safe.

I asked Eva to tell us a little more about the tiny telescope. She said it used to have a chain, attached to a hole below the big lens, and she wore it everywhere till she was in ninth grade, when the chain snagged on something and broke. Conchita had said it was so I could see her always, even far away. That last day when we were dismissed, we went straight to the schoolyard to try the telescope. We both knew even then that it couldn't see thousands of miles. But I could see her all the way across that grassy yard, with her long dark hair, pink dress and flashing smile. It did what it was meant to, it brought her close. Then we ran across the field and hugged our goodbyes.

Clint said Did you ever hear from her again? Eva poked the fire, then shook her head, said I try to forgive myself, say we were just little girls. But you know how it is. She may have lost my address. I try not to think of how it was that I never had hers. I called her house once, a week later, but the number had been disconnected. There are lessons you never want to learn about the world. How fragile love is. And how the heart was not made to see further than the eye.

No Use Ridin' in the Rain

It was overcast and cool and looked like rain, one of those early spring days that gang up on you, when before you know it you're locked outside lookin' in at trouble, where you maybe left your keys. Or else you're headed one direction, thinkin' to meet trouble halfway, when it's bound somewhere else entirely, with somethin' closer in mind.

My day had started out with an urgent call at daybreak from some decent neighbors, Sandy and Lucinda Perry, whose animals had got out. Someone with a little too much to drink or some other bee in their bonnet had run off the road in the night and plowed through their fence. The culprit had left a dented Impala dripping antifreeze in their pasture and disappeared, leaving a gaping hole for the Perrys' cattle to find. They wanted to know if I'd mind riding my horse over along the road and turn back any cattle I might come across, that were wearing their brand. It was eight miles to their place, and if I could help they'd meet up with me along the way. I asked if they'd called the Sheriff yet, because the local law had horses, rigs and trailers for just this kinda thing. Besides, they might as well haul that car away before the fence gets patched. Sandy said Good thinkin', proves I aint had my coffee yet. I said One more thing: how many head we lookin' at? Sixty a my new breedin' stock, but lucky no calves to the new batch yet.

I shook my head and muttered all the while making my own coffee and filling a travel mug, grabbed some apples and carrots and a couple granola bars to stuff in my jacket pockets, then grabbed my slicker and headed out to saddle Beulah, the best cow-herding horse on the place. Sixty full-grown animals, likely including their bull that went unmentioned, though we'd had a nodding acquaintance from a troublesome loading last year. The boys woulda been handy on a morning ride like this but they had school. I waved at the Mosleys' house as I rode by, sippin' my coffee. I'd seen Eva's light on in the kitchen, though no telling if she saw me, and no sign of the boys. Clint's truck was already long gone. I reined in at the crossroads, looked around at my big picnic table that was lookin' forlorn, and headed east. Then we loped along for nearly an hour before I saw any cattle. Then there they all were, coming at me, clopping along, all strung out, zigzagging aimlessly across the empty two-lane road. Lucky here the fences were good on both sides, and the cows were just bouncing back and forth, sampling the greenery in both ditches. I gathered my lariat up in one hand, swung it against my thigh to make a little slappin' sound, started whistling and calling to the nearest cow coming up on our left. Beulah got the idea right away, bluffed and double-clutched and turned her. As soon as we'd got that one moving the other way, we met one comin' down the double yellow line, stopped, then faked and feinted and turned her too. With two of them moving ahead of me, we met the next two on the right shoulder, waved and shouted and turned 'em back, and it started getting easier. Thirty feet up the road the cows had slowed as I pressed these first four back into them.

It was just then that the bull shouldered his way through the stalled heifers and cows, snortin', wantin' to know what was holding up the show. I aimed Beulah to cross his path at an angle, and she knew what I wanted as soon as I leaned forward in the saddle. He was already a little huffy as she feinted and stopped him, faked a second time and got a good step ahead. But when he snorted and made as if to come for us, I smacked him across the face with my lasso, shouted Back! and damn if he didn't shy away just like we wanted. The cows took the hint and fell in behind, weaving back through the traffic jam we'd started. Then a couple minutes of whoopin' and pushin' and the hard part was past, the herd all turned and headed, easing back for home.

Still, it was no picnic. These were mostly full-grown animals, new on their place, but used to throwin' their weight around. At every chance along the way, some would turn in at the driveways of neighbors, and we'd have to ride into somebody's barnyard and dig 'em out, get a few dogs riled and yappin', then get the cows all turned and moving east again along the road. The one piece of luck we had was there was no traffic. It was still a little soon for that, just past the early birds and not quite to the morning rush. I figured we still had another couple miles when I looked up and heard some shod horses clopping on blacktop out in the mists ahead. It was Sandy and Lucinda in the saddle steppin' right along. I got way over to the right, stood up in my stirrups and waved my lariat, but didn't make a sound, just drew 'em a picture with my other hand. I wanted them not to spook the cattle my way, just turn around nice and slow and let the cows ease on past 'em. We'd worked some cows like this a couple times, so they caught on quick, let the cows past then edged up alongside on their nice pair of matching roans. Lucinda said Howdy, neighbor, and Sandy said Good morning, Brick. Then he told me there was a sheriff's deputy behind me back at the crossroads, holding traffic till he got word we were clear. I suggested that the two of them might as well get ahead of the cows and be ready to turn them when we got to their place. But first tell me where you want 'em. We could run 'em in your drive and into a holding pen, if you got one free. Or shut 'em up in your barn. Otherwise they can just go back through the hole in the fence to the pasture.

They both grinned, and Sandy said You sure get to thinkin' early, neighbor. I said I brought this mare Beulah to do all my thinkin'. You shoulda seen her outfox your bull. She belongs on a dance floor, givin' lessons. They both laughed, then said they'd take 'em in the driveway straight to a spare corral. So they got up front to lead and steer, while I rode drag, and that's just what we did. Lucinda got far enough ahead to wait at the turn-offs to their neighbors' places, and keep their cows moving on the straight-an'-narrow.

When we turned in at their place and got the cattle penned, we each counted them in our heads and compared notes to make sure we had 'em all. Then I tied Beulah up with my lasso, took her bridle off, gave her an apple and a carrot. While I was at it Lucinda invited me into the house to have coffee. Sandy was calling the Sheriff to thank the deputy and tell him we were done. And if they had someone to call they could come tow that car outa the pasture. After that we had some biscuits and scrambled eggs. They said they'd been wantin' to show me some of their new breeding stock, then laughed and said Seems like you've already seen most of 'em. I said But I wasn't awake yet, so we went out to the corral and looked 'em over again in broad daylight. And while we were studyin' several of their fine new calves, the tow truck arrived, put that dented Impala up on the hook and pulled her across the field and out a sure-nuff gate so they wouldn't get stuck in that ditch where someone had drove through the fence. As soon as the tow was gone, Sandy looked like he could use a hand stretchin' some fence over that hole, so we got the tools and soon had it all good as new.

Then we opened a couple gates and hazed the cattle back out to where they belonged. By then it was along into afternoon, and startin' to drizzle so I said I gotta be gettin' on before I eat you outa house an' home.

I got the slicker off my saddle and put it on, fed Beulah the bit, stepped up and waved at the Perrys up on their porch. Then on the road home it started some serious rain, that for a while just got harder. The cars along the road had their lights on and their wipers going like crazy. We rode facing oncoming traffic but there wasn't much room on the shoulder. When we got to the crossroads there was no deputy there, but no sign of loose cattle either. I rode by the Mosleys' house, and put Beulah in the barn. It was afternoon but I didn't see sign of the boys yet, nor of Eva. I wiped the horse down and brushed her a while to dry her and say thanks. She'd put in some good work on the Perrys' cattle, so I gave her another couple carrots.

It wasn't till I got to the house to make lunch that I saw by the clock it was past time for the boys on the school bus, so I went over and knocked on the Mosleys' kitchen door. No answer. So I went back to the barn and looked around. The boys' bridles were missing, and not all the horses were there. I whistled 'em up, and saw Nokey and Lady were gone. So I tossed my saddle on Beulah, fed her the bit and buckled her throat latch, then stepped up, went out to the pasture and down the old Pipestone trail. And down at the far end there they were, two horses standing bare-backed, tails to the rain, one boy holdin' their reins, and one boy down in the mud.

I rode up and stepped down. Ike said Mr. Brick, where you been?

Never mind me, what you two been doin'? I didn't mean it to come out so rough, but I was worried. I took a couple breaths and looked the boys over. Mo had an arm stuck out at an odd angle. As I bent down my hat was drippin' in his face, so I ducked to one side.

Sorry, Mo. Looks like you got a busted wing. Are you hurt anywhere else? Did you hit your head?

Mo shook his head, but didn't make a sound. No tellin' if he'd been cryin' what with the steady rain. I took off my slicker, said I was gonna have to move him, so he needed to be brave. Then I slid it under his left side, under that bad arm that I had to straighten out a little, then folded him up in it like a taco. Then I said Here we go, Taco Man, lifted and held him close, stood up and turned around.

Ike, could you get hold of Beulah's reins too, and lead 'em all to the barn? When you get there climb up on a gate an' slip off their bridles, and I'll get Beulah's saddle off when I got a free hand. Then you need to open the back door of the truck so I can slide Mo in. We're gonna take him to the hospital, and we're gonna need some pillows and the blanket off my couch to warm him up and keep him from rollin' around.

Neither of the boys said much more till we got all that done. Mo was trembling and twitching a little, and I tried not to hold him too tight and yet keep him still. It was the better part of two miles back to the barn, and by the end I was huffin' an' shakin' both. And we were all soaked to the skin. As I laid Mo in the back seat out flat, I leaned close and said How you doin', pardner, and seemed like he whispered Better now they shut off the rain. I left a little room for Ike to sit by his head and hold him from rolling while I drove. Then Ike got the pillows and blanket while I tossed the saddle off of Beulah. I asked Ike if he knew where his mom was. He said she left a note saying she had a doctor appointment but would be home later to make supper, so we should come give you a hand. Her note said she saw you ride out before we got up this morning, but figured you'd be back by the time the school bus dropped us off. I went back to the house to get my cell phone, which I didn't have much use for, just bought for emergencies when I was out in the field or off traveling. Then I asked if the boys knew their parents' phone numbers, and they both did, so we were off.

It started raining again, on into town and out the far side, to the little hospital we had. I drove around to the emergency entrance and pulled in close, turned on the flashers then went in and said we had a boy out in the truck with a broken arm. The receptionist said How'd it happen, and I said the boys haven't told me yet. I think he fell off a horse. So they brought out a board with handles round the edges, slid him on it and lifted him out onto a gurney, then wheeled him inside. I told Mo I would call his parents and they'd be here soon as they could. Otherwise he and Ike would be having dinner with me, so not to worry. And you're a brave boy, but you're 'sposed to say Ouch when it hurts, so we'll know not to move you like that.

Ike and I went out to park the truck, then came back to the waiting room, where I got him to write down his parents' phone numbers. Then we went out in the hall to make some calls. I said I'd just tell them what happened and let you talk to them. I said Who should we call first? Mom, he said. So I dialed her, and when she answered, I said Eva, it's Brick. We got a little situation here. Mo broke his arm, so we brought him to the hospital. She said Is he gonna be all right? I said Far as I can tell. Here's Ike, he wants to talk to you.

Ike said Hi Mom, then did a little listening. When he got his chance he talked about them out riding bareback, looking for me in the big pasture, when it started raining hard. They were both having trouble hanging on, and decided to go back and wait in the barn. When they turned uphill Mo slipped off sideways and landed under Lady's feet. The mare reared off to one side and didn't step on him, but he'd landed smack on his arm and broke it. Then she got to hear how I found them and rolled Mo up in my slicker, carried him back and put him in the truck.

Eva asked to speak to me then, said she would call Clint and have him come get her and meet us at the emergency waiting room. I asked if she could think of anything else to do at this end, and she said Give those boys a hug and say we'll be there soon. And thank you for lookin' after 'em. Lord knows it ain't always easy.

Clint and Eva walked in an hour later, and didn't have long to wait before the nurse called out Mosley, and said we could come get Mo in a minute, but the doctor wanted to talk to us first. We stepped out in the hall and there was Doctor Melanie Brooks, a tall Black woman who looked like she mighta been a basketball star before med school. She said Mo appeared to have a bump over his left ear from his fall, but the CAT-scan showed no signs of fracture or concussion, and he seemed fine apart from his broken arm. He was upset that we'd had to cut up the slicker to get it off him, and complained that he lost his hat somewhere. He seemed upset that somebody named Mr. Brick might be mad, and said it wasn't Lady's fault, she just slipped in the mud. Other than that Mo is a perfect patient. I'd like to see him in six weeks to see how he's healing. The cast ought to be on for twelve weeks, give or take. If you have any problems with pain, headaches or blurry vision or signs of infection--streaky redness or swelling-- be sure to call me or your pediatrician right away.

Then we went in and gathered up Mo. Eva squeezed him so hard she like to broke his other arm. Clint told her to take it easy, he was safe now. Mo told me he was sorry they had to cut up my slicker, and hoped I wasn't mad. I said That old one leaked anyhow. You had me worried, not mad. I just had on my serious face. No reason you'da seen it before, what with all our jokin', but now you know how that looks, so needn't wonder.

By the time we pulled up at the ranch the rain had about quit for good, and it was gettin' on toward evening. I parked the truck in the shed and thought I'd go find that boy's hat and see was it wrecked or just got some more character. By the time I tossed my saddle on Lucky there was Ike askin' where I was goin'. I said Go get Beulah and we'll saddle her so you can go too. So we did, and in the twilight we rode down, slipped and slid a little but located Mo's hat with a flashlight, that was not too bad, had just got stepped on a little, needed to dry out with some wadded newspaper inside, and in a day or two might hold still to brush the dry mud off. Then we switched off the light, turned around and let Beulah lead us the way to the barn.

I'd sent Ike in for supper, and took the gear off the horses, then fed and watered 'em. When I handed Mo's hat to Eva at the kitchen door, that I'd wadded with newspaper, I told her If I'da known what the day would bring I'da dropped in and had coffee first thing and let it wait. At least then you'da known where to find me. She said Likewise and vice-a-versa. I couldn't go without saying You know, those are some awful good boys. And she said No doubt of it, and turned away. I went home and thawed out two chicken pot pies for lunch an' supper, ate 'em both in my bathrobe, spread my clothes out to dry on the kitchen chairs, crawled in bed early, and let the Mosleys be. I knew they had plenty to chew on, with a couple boys who prob'ly needed a little reassurance, peace and quiet. I fell asleep picturing Mo as a chirping little bird layin' there in the mud with a busted wing.

The next day was clear, and gettin' on for spring. I saw Ike standin' out waitin' for the school bus alone, so Mo must be takin' the day off. I was tryin' to think how to tell 'em what was on my mind, but I waited all day, just doin' chores, cleanin' up and putterin' around. Clint walked over after work and asked if I'd like to have dinner with 'em. Turned out that we were grillin' some little tiny hamburgers they called slammers or sliders, and que-sadillas that Mo and all the rest of us could manage to eat with one hand.

After we polished off our little one-handed dinners, Clint tossed a few logs on the coals and stirred up a fire. I asked Mo if I could have a look at his arm, just checkin' bruises and coloring. Really wanted to see for my-self if Lady had stepped on him, but it looked like she'd missed. While I was at it Mo told me what his doctor Melanie Brooks had said before she came out in the hall, how when that bone heals it'll be the strongest bone in your body, and will never break there again. Though I don't know that I believe that. I said I think what she said is the gospel. Never seen a bone to break twice the same place on anyone. When I asked how he was feeling, he said his arm was tingly, and his fingers too. It still hurt but not so much. Said he was gettin' used to havin' it in a sling, an' doin' things with one hand. I said What's the hardest thing? He said Wipin' my butt. An' gettin' toothpaste on the toothbrush. I reached in my pocket and handed him a bundle of differ-ent colored markers with a rubber band, so he could get the kids at school to decorate his cast. I said What do you remember about what happened? He said It all went by so quick. That mare Lady was slippery as all get-out. Like Mom's sliders on the griddle. But Lady didn't step on me. She was right there slippin' too, but somehow got outa the way. Then I crash-landed, got awful cold but couldn't get up. Couldn't move. Reckon I's just too scared. My teeth were clackin' and clatterin' so loud I thought they might break.

That's okay, Mo. You know what the old hands say: No use ridin' in the rain unless you got somewhere to be that don't mind if you come in late an' wet. Otherwise wait till the rain lets up. The horses mostly don't care, but it sure can put a rider in a fix. I hadn't ever told you boys how to ride bareback, but here it is: you need to grab onto the horse's mane above the withers and really dig your fingers in, take a good hold. Their hair is really strong. And dig your heels in her sides. But the real reason I never told you was because I reckoned those big heavy saddles would make you wait to grow up. And that was my mistake.

I need to say something, and it's not to hurt your feelings, but you boys shouldn't a been out there--we all know that. It was bad conditions, no good for bareback ridin' which they mostly do in a circus tent, an' make you pay to watch. You're both smart and fearless, know just about everything you need to, already. You're just not big enough yet. There's still things you shouldn't try till you get a little more size an' muscle, like shoeing and trim-ming horses' hooves. You already got the attitude right, I can see that. I've known cowboys who knew less than you get all crippled up because horses stepped on 'em, kicked 'em, bit 'em. Those were hands who treated their horses like equipment, or like dirt. Muscled 'em around, pushed and pulled 'em, shouted, had no patience. It's no surprise to me that Lady got outa the way when you fell. She was in a bad spot herself, but did what she could. She was thinkin' about you 'cause you're always thinkin' about her, what she likes an' needs. That's what a real cowboy does.

I stopped then to catch air a minute. Then stood up to say what I had to. I looked around at the Mosleys, who were all quiet. The sky was clearing to blue-black, showing the first stars. I said I got two little stories to tell, about growing up the hard way. At least hard for this one.

When I was your age I remember once for a whole year craving to ride my horse to school. I even planned where to tie her, in a patch of shade at the end of the ball field, and worked out how to take her bridle off and put a halter and lead rope on her for the day, so I could stake her out where she could eat a little grass. But the Moon Dog Ranch was thirty miles from school, and I'd of had to get up two hours early, sneak out and ride hard all the way to make it by first bell. The roads were narrow, with hardly room on the shoulder for a bicycle, much less a horse and rider--about like that road out to the Perrys' place yesterday. I wanted to ride my horse and leave her tied where my classmates--and one girl in particular--could see her out the window all day long. I was sure my horse would be irresistible, and all the cute girls would want to come pet her and feed her at lunch time. I thought about it and planned it endlessly. The one thing I couldn't figure out was how to get the saddle on her, and cinch it tight. I was ten, a little younger than Mo is now, and I was practicing swinging my old saddle around with my arms, and booting it up overhead with my knee. I was getting there, but wasn't there quite yet. I just wasn't tall enough and strong enough, and couldn't wait till I was. Out in our barn there was a box stall with a top rail that was just the height of my horse's back, that I'd practice on. When I'd go out to do chores after supper, I'd do half a dozen tosses every night. The horses got tired of hearin' me tossin' that poor saddle up, and hear it come crashin' down.

Of course that wasn't the whole story, not by a long shot. It never is. Here's the thing. I wasn't doin' all that well in school. I could do the stuff they wanted me to do, read and write and figure numbers, but didn't much want to, and wasn't havin' much fun. So I didn't try very hard. I just wanted to be outside doing what the hands on the ranch did, that was a little different every day. It wasn't all fun, it was mostly work, but those were things I already knew how to do. Stuff like herding, and mending fence, bucking hay and mucking out the stalls. I figured in a year or two I'd get big enough to toss a saddle over the chimney if I wanted, or pick up a newborn calf and lay her over my saddle, and carry her up to the barn to find her mama--then I'd be set to quit school. I even saw it wasn't so much the riding to school I daydreamed about, but the saying goodbye and the riding away. See, for most of those kids school was an escape from home, a way to see the world and go find work an' adventure in the big city. But I'd thought of all that, and saw the school that led to it like it was a long row of cages, and each fall in a new class I felt exactly the same--silly and trapped, as each cage opened into the next. I thought most of what they had me doing was a waste of time. It wasn't really a waste, but that's how it seemed to this boy who just wanted to be a cowhand. I learned I was wrong when I got out of high school and went straight in the Army, that had no room or time at all for cowboys. But I soon found out I liked to learn things, and pretty soon wanted to know everything. I even took some college courses when I got back from Vietnam that gave me endless stuff to think about, and made me feel not so alone.

The boys were quiet, poking the fire, and Clint and Eva were quiet too. They couldn't see where this was heading. So I thought I'd better just get it done. I said You've all been my friends a good while now, and I hope this will make sense. I was born onto a big ranch, that turned into a strange place. When I was four, my mama died of influenza from what they called complications, that made no sense at all. I hardly remember her. If it wasn't for a couple pictures I got put away, I wouldn't know her to talk to in broad daylight. When she died, my father backed off, didn't have much to do with me and my little sister Kathleen, so my grandfather took over. I never met my grandmother, I only heard stories. She was dead before my time. My grandfather hired a sweet Mexican woman Elena to cook and look after my little sister and me. She had the most beautiful voice, and would sing us to sleep at night if we'd been good. Her songs were all Spanish, sad and magical. But when I was five and a half, I snuck out of bed to the top of the stairs one night, and heard Grampa and my dad talking about the ranch, how hard it was to make a go of. And Grampa said he had a plan, to drill for oil on the place. A couple of big companies had approached him, interested in drilling test wells. And my father just went along, didn't really care. He was drinking a lot, couldn't seem to help himself, and anyone could see he was having no fun. But then he went right along with whatever the old man wanted. After all, it was his ranch, his say-so, and he was planning on living forever.

From that night on I was on the lookout for any sign of the oil people and what they might do. The ranch was 218,000 acres, over 340 square miles. We prob'ly had a hundred horses right then, and a couple or three thousand cows. There was a foreman, a cook, and a dozen full-time hands, and we'd hire more for spring and fall roundup. For a boy like me the Moon Dog ranch might as well a been cowboy heaven, even if it never made a nickel.

Then one afternoon a big silver-haired man with a red face dressed in a fancy cowboy rig drove up in a powder-blue Cadillac. He had on a big white hat and a silver suit, polished black boots and a fancy shirt with pearl buttons and a big shiny turquoise stone under his chin on his bolo tie. He had a briefcase with an oil company logo. My little sister Kathleen and I were up on the porch on the glider, swinging back and forth in the shade. The man climbed the steps, looked over and asked if Mr. Whittaker was at home. I just sat and stared at him.

What are you little rascals up to? What's the matter, cat got your tongue?

I couldn't guess what a rascal might be, but didn't care for the sound of it. I still didn't say a word, just jumped up and ran straight past him over to the front door, snatched up the brick they kept there for a door-stop, and threw it at his big old baby-blue car. It hit with a clunk an' put a big dent in the trunk lid. Just then Elena the housekeeper came to the door, with my dad right on her heels, and they got to see the man run down the steps, jump in his car and tear off.

Well, I got sent to bed without supper, and they didn't say a word to me till late the next day. In the meantime somebody started calling me Brick, most likely one a the cowboys, an' it stuck. My real name is Brian. Grampa and my dad were both hoppin' mad at losin' this chance. Lucky for them there's more than one oil company that loves the stink of oil money bein' made. But ever since from that day to this I been Brick. Turned out that brick I threw was a special one, that came from when Grampa's country schoolhouse was torn down, back in the 1940s. A little square one-room place with coathooks and shelves in the back, with blackboards and benches and a stove in the middle. The cowhands said it was the one thing on the place older than he was. Seems I chipped a corner off it, that they never could find to glue back. But I got to pay to fix that oil man's car, that took almost two years of chores at five dollars a week, an' no one turned loose or let me forget for a minute. The bill for that dent was $256. And after the wells got drilled and the pump jacks set up and the money commenced to flowin', they looked around and noticed they'd pretty much quit ranchin', though they still had the barns an' stables, an' horses an' cows. So they built some fancy new cabins and set up for dude ranchin'. Your parents prob'ly know what that is, though no reason why you should. It's when city folks pay by the week to come out to a ranch an' play cowboy. Some of 'em need the best kind of horse to put up with 'em, and still never get a clue.

Throwin' that brick is really the only bad thing I've ever done, and I still don't know what got into me. Protectin' something, fightin' something else. But it was so impulsive and mysterious, even to this little boy watching in the shadows before he hardly knew he had a self. Maybe a self is just a shell you build up on the outside, to hold the seed of what you hope is alive, before it gets planted, that keeps out the ugly world that threatens to snuff out the little spark that might grow into you given time, given rain an' nourishment.

Over the long haul it seems like they never forgave me and wouldn't let me into their club, even when I was running my own little Pipestone spread, and by some miracle had found Muncie. When we went and got married, they came to our wedding, but didn't want to, and left the party early. It's like they were always expecting another brick to come whistlin' through the air at 'em, like here was one more mean horse gone wrong, that could never be trusted to ground-tie or work cattle in a hackamore.

With that I was done and shut my mouth and sat down. But then Eva stood up and spoke up. She made me remember why there are things you have to stand to say, to give 'em room. She said she had planned to tell us some news yesterday, but it looked like we all needed a little quiet mending first. She said I had got stuck and didn't know what to do when I got a call that they needed to see me right away, and realized we'd been depending on Mr. Brick being around and helping out with everything. And with you boys both growing up so fast, maybe we got out ahead of ourselves. I apologize for that. You had sixty cows--or fifty-nine cows and a bull--out in the road miles away, and some other folks counting on you too when things got tough. I think we're all lucky and oughta be grateful. So from all of us, thank you, Mr. Brick. And call yourself whatever you like best, and we'll just call you that too. But as it is, if we took a vote I bet we'd all like Mr. Brick, that suits you fine an' feels like you musta grown into it, made it bigger and stronger than they thought it could ever be when you were small.

But now for a little news better late than never. I saw my doctor yesterday. Had to go in for a test, an ultrasound. And found out we're gonna have a baby. And it's gonna be a girl. So I have to ask you all to get set for the ride, and don't be too hard on her--welcome her an' give her a hand up in the saddle when she comes. 'Cause I suspect that'll be where she feels like she belongs.

Author's Note

When I was little, waiting out WWII at my grandparents' general store in rural Indiana, it wasn't long before I was studying horses every chance I got--their whiskery long faces and velvet noses, their shy knowing ways and steady skeptical eyes. How they tipped an ear and cocked a hoof to stand awhile. How they pissed hard and long, and pooped indifferently, lifting a tail in the midst of whatever they did. How they romped and frolicked on a bright spring morning, playing colts and foals again. How their lips fluttered, stealing a fresh taste of whatever offered, no matter where they were tied.

For a while horses still seemed to be everywhere, and my uncle Edwin's mismatched work team was a model of all that was right with that world--how Duke and Bill could pull a truck or tractor out of any ditch. How they would shake the ground under my feet as they flopped down and rolled after being unhitched and unbuckled from working a long day in harness, wagging their silver hooves in the lavender air as the last swallows stole a sip from their trough on the wing, then looped and screeled toward the barn.

My first clue about riding horses came from my uncle Edwin's mule, Queenie, who was so smart she could read grownup minds. Edwin said we could ride her if she would let us, so one of the older brothers saddled and bridled her, then these four little kids in a row, two aged five and two six, piled on. Queenie swung her head around to study us, then set off around the pasture at a stately stroll. We kids scrunched and kicked a little, sawed the reins and yelled as if to play cowboys, but nothing changed. Luckily we had no control over the mule who was already ancient, still employed to till the garden patch since only she could be counted on never to step on a living thing. When she got back to the shed where she'd started, she stopped to let us kids scramble down, and we did. A lifetime later that mule's intelligent care for us remains a source of astonishment. We treated her like a ride; she treated us like a treasure.

CPSIA information can be obtained
at www.ICGtesting.com
Printed in the USA
BVHW040802280322
632624BV00013B/63